Bjørnstjerne Bjørnson

The Bridal March

Captain Mansana

Bjørnstjerne Bjørnson

The Bridal March
Captain Mansana

ISBN/EAN: 9783337155551

Printed in Europe, USA, Canada, Australia, Japan

Cover: Foto ©ninafisch / pixelio.de

More available books at **www.hansebooks.com**

THE BRIDAL MARCH

CAPTAIN MANSANA

WORKS OF
BJÖRNSTJERNE BJÖRNSON

PATRIOTS EDITION

THE BRIDAL MARCH

CAPTAIN MANSANA

Translated from the Norse

By

RASMUS B. ANDERSON

NEW YORK
DOUBLEDAY, PAGE & COMPANY

THE BRIDAL MARCH

PREFACE.

"THE Bridal March" (Brudeslaatten) was published in 1872, and was dedicated to Hans Christian Andersen, the celebrated Danish story-teller. This is the last of the author's peasant novels, and he will probably never produce another. He has become more and more deeply interested in the great social and political questions of the century, and the stories and dramas he now writes are imbued with the progressive spirit of the age.

The four striking illustrations in this volume were made expressly for "The Bridal March" by Norway's most distinguished *genre* painter, Adolf Tidemand, who was born in 1814 and died in 1876. He made a specialty of illustrating the character, customs, and manners of Norwegian country life, and in this field of art he has never been equaled by any other Scandinavian painter. His delineation of faces, interiors, the every-day life, and the solemnities and festivities of the Norwegian peasantry, secured him the admiration of the world, and are as faithful to reality as one of Björnson's peasant stories. I doubt not that the four illustrations by Tidemand in this volume will be studied with as much pleasure as the story itself.

RASMUS B. ANDERSON.

ASGARD, MADISON, WISCONSIN,
    May, 1882.

THE BRIDAL MARCH.

There dwelt in one of the larger mountain valleys of Norway, some time during the last century, a fiddler, whose name after him passed, in a measure, into legendary lore. Quite an array of songs and dances are ascribed to him; some of these, according to tradition, he learned from the underground folk, one from the Evil One himself, one he made for the purpose of saving his life, etc. One of his tunes has become famous beyond all the others, for its history did not end with his life, it really began after he was dead.

The fiddler, Ole Haugen, a poor houseman living far up the mountain, had a daughter named Aslaug, who had inherited his fine head and his musical talent, if not for playing at least for everything else of the same nature; for she was easy and self-possessed in conversation, in singing, in her walk, and in dancing; and had, too, a very flexible voice, a common thing in her family. The third son of the ancient house of Tingvold, a young man, returned from distant lands. His two brothers, both of them older than he, had been drowned in a freshet, and he was now heir to the gard. He met Aslaug at a large wedding-party and fell in love with her. It was an unheard-of thing in those days for a gardman's son of so old and prominent a family to woo one in Aslaug's circumstances and rank of life. This young man, however, had been long absent from home, and he gave his parents to understand that he had ample means abroad for his support; if he could not have what he wanted at home, he said, it mattered little to him what became of the gard. It was universally prophesied that such disregard of his family and the inheritance of his forefathers, would bring its own punishment; it was said, too, that Ole Haugen must have influenced him, and perhaps with help that every mortal should fear.

While the struggle between the young man and his parents was going on, Ole Haugen, so it is stated, had been in the most excellent spirits. But when the victory was won, he is said to have announced that he had already made a bridal march for the young couple; it could never by any possibility be lost to the house of Tingvold; but Heaven have mercy on the bride, he is furthermore charged with having said, who did not drive to church to its strains with as happy a heart as that of the houseman's daughter from Haugen! And this led people to suspect some evil influence.

This is the tradition, and it is like so many others. But something more reliable than tradition is the fact, that in this as well as in other mountain parishes there exists, even to the present day, a lively taste for music and ballads, and in past times it must have been still keener. Such tastes can only be preserved through those who are able to enlarge and embellish the inherited treasure-stores, and Ole Haugen certainly possessed this power to a remarkable degree.

Tradition states, furthermore, that as Ole Haugen's bridal march was the most joyous one that had ever been heard, so the first bride and groom that drove home to its music, after having been conducted by the same to the church door, and met there again by the glad sounds at the conclusion of the ceremony, were the happiest couple that had ever been seen And although the Tingvold family had always been a handsome race, and after this time became still more noted for its beauty, yet legendary lore stoutly asserts that this bridal pair must carry off the palm through all coming generations.

We pass now from tradition to firmer ground; for with Ole Haugen legendary lore dies; after him history begins. The latter tells us that this bridal march became an heir-loom in the family, differing from other heir-looms, which seldom are of any use; for this *was used*, that is to say, the tune was sung, shouted, whistled, tooted, played from house to stable, from the home-fields to the woodland pasture; and to its glad strains the only child the couple ever had was rocked and dandled in the arms of its mother, its father, the nurse-maid, and the rest of the household servants; and the first thing it learned after its earliest tricks and words was the bridal march. The child was called Astrid. There was music in the family, and particularly in this sprightly little girl, who could soon sing with a tra-la-la, in a masterly way, the bridal march, the victory shout of her parents, the promise of her family. It was, indeed, no wonder that when she was grown up she insisted upon making her own choice of a lover. Perhaps rumor has exaggerated the number of Astrid's suitors; but one thing is certain : this wealthy girl, with her refined nature, when over twenty-three years of age, was not yet betrothed. Then at last the cause of this came to light! Several years before her mother had taken in from the highway a bright gypsy lad; he was not really a gypsy lad, but was called so, and especially by Astrid's mother when it reached her ears that her daughter and he had most strangely entered into a betrothal up in the woodland pasture, and that now they passed their time in singing the bridal march to each other, she from the store-house roof, he from the slope above. The youth was quickly sent away; for now it appeared that no one held more strictly to the "family" than the former houseman's daughter. And the father could not help thinking of the prophecy made when he himself violated the customs of his family. They of the house of Tingvold were already giving their children in marriage to people from the highway. Where would this end? The parish did not judge more leniently. The gypsy lad — Knut was his name — had taken to trading, especially in cattle, and was known to every one. He was the first person in this parish, indeed for miles round, who had gone into the business on so large a scale. He opened this avenue of trade, and thus procured for the parishes better prices for their stock, and increased the wealth of many a family. But this did not prevent carousing and fighting from following in his footsteps wherever he went, and this was the only thing that people talked about; for his worth as a trader they did not yet understand. By the time Astrid was twenty-three years old, it had become pretty evident that either the gard must pass out of the direct line of descent, or this man would have to be taken into it; for Astrid's parents had, through their own marriage, lost the moral power which might have enabled them to take compulsory measures. So Astrid had her way: the lively, handsome Knut drove to church with her one fine day, at the head of an immense procession. The bridal march of the house of Tingvold, the grandfather's masterpiece, flashed back over the train of followers, and the young couple sat as though they were joining in the merry tune with a low tra-la-la, for they looked very blithe and gay. People were astonished to see that the parents also seemed in good spirits; they had made such long and persevering resistance.

After the wedding, Knut undertook the management of the farm, and the old people had a yearly allowance made them; but this was so large that no one could understand how Knut

and Astrid were able to afford it; for although
the gard was the largest in the parish, it was
far from being in a good condition. Nor was
this all; the working force was increased threefold, and new methods were introduced at an
expense hitherto unheard of in that region.
Certain ruin was predicted for him. But the
"gypsy lad," as Knut was still called, maintained his cheerfulness, and his high spirits in-
'ected Astrid. The delicate, shy maiden of
yore had become a stirring, robust housewife.
Her parents were consoled. At last people
began to find out that Knut had brought to
Tingvold what no one had had there before:
capital for carrying on the farming! He had,
moreover, brought large experience from his
rambling life, besides a faculty for handling
merchandise and money, and for keeping laborers and servants good-natured and cheerful;
and so at the end of twelve years Tingvold
could scarcely have been recognized. The
houses were entirely changed, the farm stock
was increased threefold, and was three times
better kept than before, and Knut himself in a
dress-coat, with a "meerschaum pipe," and a
glass of toddy, passed his evenings with the
captain, the priest, and the lensmand. Astrid
adored him as the wisest and best man on earth,

and she herself told that in his youth he now and
then got into fights and drank too much, simply
that rumors of his doings might reach her ears
and alarm her; "for he was such a shrewd fellow." She followed his example in everything,
except in making a change in her dress and
habits; she preferred keeping to the peasant
customs and dress. Knut always allowed others
to follow their own inclinations; and so no discord entered his home because of Astrid's
wishes. He lived his own way and she waited
on him. It was a frugal life he led, be it observed; he was too sensible to care to make a
great noise or to incur heavy expense. Some
said that he made at card-playing, and through
the importance and associations it opened to
him, *more* than it cost him to live; but this
was doubtless mere scandal.

They had several children, whose history does
not concern us; but the eldest son, Endrid, who
was to succeed to the gard, was also expected
to increase its honors. He was handsome, like
all the rest of his family; but his mind was
only adapted to common-place affairs, as may
often be observed in the children of enterprising parents. His father early noticed this,
and resolved to supply the boy's deficiencies
through a superior education. For this reason

the children had a private tutor; and Endrid, when grown, was sent to one of the agricultural schools, which at this time were just being improved, and later to the city. He came home again a quiet boy, who showed marks of overstudy, and who had fewer city habits than could have been anticipated, or than his father desired. Endrid was, in fact, by no means quick at learning.

Numerous were the speculations made on this boy, both by the captain and the priest, each of whom had several daughters; but if this were the cause of the increased consideration they showed Knut, they deceived themselves very badly indeed, for Knut so thoroughly despised a marriage with a poor captain's or priest's daughter, who was without preparation for the management of the affairs of a large gard, that he did not even deem it worth his while to warn his son. Nor was it needful that he should: the young man saw as clearly as he that the family required something more than merely being raised to prosperity, and that it must now mingle with the blood of those who were its equals in age and respectability. But the misfortune was that the youth was somewhat awkward when he went on his matrimonial errands, and people mistrusted him.

This might not have made so much difference had he not gained the reputation of being on the lookout for a good match, and peasants are always shy of one of whom such things are said. Endrid himself soon noticed this; for if he was not very shrewd, he was, on the other hand, extremely sensitive. He perceived that it in nowise bettered his situation that he had the clothes and manners of the city, as people said. And as at bottom there was something really worthy in this boy, the effect of his mortification was that he gradually laid aside his city dress and city speech and set to work on his father's immense gard, like any common laborer. His father understood it all; indeed, he knew before the young man understood it himself, and he begged the boy's mother not to appear to notice anything. Therefore they said nothing to their son about marriage, and no further heed was paid to the change which had taken place in him, than that his father, with ever-increasing kindness of manner, admitted him to his plans about the farming and other family concerns, and gradually placed the entire management of the gard in his son's hands. He never had cause to regret having done so.

Thus matters stood with the son until he was thirty-one years old, having increased his father's property and his own experience and prudence. During all this time he had made no attempt, no, not the slightest, to court any of the girls in or out of the parish, and now his parents began to grow seriously uneasy lest he had entirely put marriage out of his head. But this he had not done.

In the neighboring gard there lived, in good circumstances, a family of the best blood in the parish, and one that had several times, too, intermarried with the ancient house of Tingvold. There grew up there a young girl, in whom Endrid had taken an interest from the time she was a little child; very likely he had in secret set his heart on her, for only half a year after her confirmation he offered himself to her. She was seventeen years old, he thirty-one. Randi, that was her name, could not at once nake up her mind what answer she should give 1im; she went to her parents about it, but they told her they would leave it entirely to herself. They thought Endrid was a most worthy man, and that, as far as property went, this was the best match she could make. The difference in age was great, and she must herself decide whether she, young as she was, had the courage to assume the responsibilities of the large gard and the many unfamiliar duties. Randi knew very well that her parents would rather have her say Yes than No; but she was really alarmed. So she went over to see Endrid's mother, whom she had always liked. She took it for granted that his mother knew of his suit, but found to her astonishment that she knew nothing about it. The good mother was so delighted that she used all her powers of persuasion to induce Randi to say Yes.

"I will help you," said she. "Father will not accept any annuity; he has his own means, and he does not want his children to grudge him his life. There will at once be a general division of the property, and the little which we shall hereafter have for our support will then be divided after we are gone. From this you can judge that you will not be taking on yourself any annoyances so far as we are concerned."

Yes, Randi knew very well that Astrid and Knut were kind.

"And our boy," continued Astrid, "is good and considerate."

Yes, Randi had learned that for herself; she was not afraid of getting on with him — if she were only worthy herself.

A few days later the matter was settled, and if Endrid was happy, so too were his parents for he was about to marry into a highly-esteemed family, and the girl herself was so pretty and so sensible that in those respects there had perhaps never been a better match in the parish. The old people of both families conferred together about the wedding, which was arranged to take place just before harvest, for there was no occasion for waiting in this case.

The parish, meanwhile, did not receive these tidings in the same manner as the parties interested. It was thought that the pretty young girl had " sold herself." She was so young that she could scarcely know what marriage meant, and the wily Knut had no doubt urged his son on before the girl was as yet ready for suitors. A little of this talk reached Randi's ears, but Endrid was so affectionate, and that in such a quiet, almost humble way, that she would not break with him, yet she grew rather cold. The parents of both had no doubt also heard one thing and another, but acted as though all were well.

The marriage was to be celebrated in grand style, perhaps just to defy gossip, and for that same reason the preparations were not displeasing to Randi. Knut's associates, the priest, the captain, and the lensmand, with the whole of their large families, were to accompany the bridal party to church. That was why Knut did not wish any fiddling — it was too old-fashioned and countrified; but Astrid insisted that the bridal march of the family must conduct the young couple to church and thence back home again; they had been too happy with it themselves, she said, not to have the satisfaction of enjoying its repetition on the marriage day of their dear children. Knut did not trouble himself much about poetry and things of that sort; he let his wife settle the matter. A hint was given to the bride's parents, therefore, that the fiddlers might be engaged, and the old march, which had been allowed to rest for a while, because the present representatives of the family worked without song, was requested.

The wedding day unfortunately set in with a furious autumnal rain. The fiddlers were forced to cover up their instruments after having played the party out of the gard, and they did not bring them forth again until they had gone far enough to hear the church-bells ringing. A boy was obliged to stand behind them on the cart holding an umbrella over them, and beneath it they sat huddled together, scraping away. The march did not sound well in such weather, as might be expected, neither did the bridal party that followed look happy. The bridegroom had his wedding hat tucked away between his knees, and a southwester on his head; he had a large leathern jacket drawn over his shoulders, and he held an umbrella over the bride, who had kerchief upon kerchief wrapped about her to protect her crown and the rest of her finery, and who had rather the appearance of a hay-mow than a human being. Thus they drove on, cart after cart, the men dripping, the women bundled up and concealed from view; it was a mysterious sort of a bridal party, in which not a face could be seen or recognized, only a quantity of rolled up heaps of wool or fur stowed closely together. The unusually great throng that had gathered along the road-side to see the wealthy bridal party pass by had to laugh, at first in suppressed tones, but finally louder and louder, as each cart passed. Near the large house where the party had to alight to arrange their dress before entering the church, a peddler, a droll fellow, whose name was Aslak, was standing on a hay-cart which had driven out of the way into the corner by the shed. Just as the bride was being lifted out of the cart, he shouted, —

"The deuce a bit will Ole Haugen's bridal march sound to-day!"

A laugh arose in the crowd, and the almost universal effort to suppress this only made it the more apparent what every one thought and was striving to conceal.

When the kerchiefs were removed from the bride, they saw that she was as white as a sheet. She wept, tried to laugh, then wept again, and then all at once she took it into her head that she would not go to church! Amid the commotion that now followed, she had to be laid down on a bed in a side-room, for she was seized with a fit of weeping that alarmed every one. Her worthy parents stood by, and when she implored them to spare her from going into church, they said that she must do as she pleased. Then her eyes sought Endrid. Any one so unhappy, aye, so utterly helpless, she had never seen, for to him there had been truth in their compact. At his side stood his mother; she said nothing and not a muscle of her face moved. But tear after tear trickled down her cheeks; her eyes hung on Randi's. At last Randi raised herself up on her elbows, stared for a while right before her, sobbing through her tears, and presently she said, —

"Oh yes! I will go to church."

Then flinging herself back on the pillow again, she wept for a time, bitterly; but after this she rose. Later she added, that she did not want any more music, and she was allowed to have her way. But the dismissed fiddlers did not improve the story when they mingled with the crowd outside.

It was a sorry bridal procession which now moved toward the church. The rain, of course, permitted the bride and bridegroom to hide their faces from the curiosity of the multitude until they entered the church; but they felt that they were running the gauntlet and that their own large company were ill pleased at having been deluded into taking part in such a fool's errand.

The famous fiddler, Ole Haugen, was buried close by the church door. By common consent his grave had been protected: one of his family had placed a new head-board there, as the old one had decayed around the bottom. The head-board was shaped like a wheel at the top, Ole himself had left orders to have it so. The grave was on a sunny spot, and countless wild flowers grew there. Every church-goer that had ever stood by this grave, knew, from one source or another, that a man who at state expense had been collecting plants and flowers in the surrounding villages and mountains, had found flowers on this grave which did not grow for miles around. The effect was, that the peasants who usually cared little for what they called " weeds," felt an inquisitive delight in these flowers, perhaps too, an inquisitive shyness; some of the flowers were uncommonly pretty. Now as the bridal pair walked past this grave, Endrid, who held Randi by the hand, noticed that a shudder ran through her; for it seemed to her that Ole Haugen's ghost had been walking to-day. Immediately afterward her tears began to flow again, consequently she entered the church weeping, and was led weeping to her seat. Thus no bride had been known to come into this church in the memory of man.

Randi felt, as she sat there, that she was now confirming the rumor that was afloat about her having been sold. The terrible disgrace to her parents that there was in this, caused her to grow cold and for a while to be able to restrain her tears. But at the altar she became agitated again over some remark or other of the priest, and at once all that she had experienced this day rushed upon her; it seemed to her for a time as though she could never look people in the eyes again, least of all her parents.

All the rest is but a repetition of what we have been over, and therefore there is nothing further to report except that she could not sit down to dinner with the company, and when entreaties and threats brought her to the supper-table she spoiled all pleasure there and had to be taken to bed. The wedding party that was to have lasted several days, broke up that same evening. "The bride was ill," it was announced.

Although no one believed this, it was, nevertheless, but too true. Randi was no longer well, nor was she ever very hearty again. And one of the results was that the first child of this couple was sickly. The love of the parents for this little one was naturally none the less devoted, because they both understood that they were, in a certain way, responsible for its suffering. They associated with no one except this child; to church they never went; they were afraid of people. For two years God granted them their happiness with their child, and then He took this too.

The first clear thought they could command after this blow was that they had been too fond of the child. That was why they had lost it. And so when another child was born unto them, it seemed as if neither of them dared bestow much affection on it. But the child, who in the beginning appeared as sickly as the first, revived, and became much more sprightly than the other had been, so that its charms were irresistible. A new, pure joy entered their hearts; they could forget what had befallen them when they were with their child. When the little one was two years old, God took it also.

There are some people who are singled out by sorrow. They are just the very ones who seem to us *least* to need it, but they are, nevertheless, best fitted to bear testimony of faith and self-denial. This couple had early sought God together; henceforth their sole communion was with Him. There had long been a hush over life at Tingvold, now it became like a church before the priest enters. Work went on undisturbed, but between every hour of labor Endrid and Randi had a little time of devotion, in which they communed with those on the other side. It caused no change when, shortly after the last loss, Randi gave birth to a daughter; the two children who had died were sons, and a girl was for this reason hardly acceptable to the parents. Moreover, they knew not if she would be spared to them. But the health and happiness the mother had enjoyed just before the loss of the last boy had been of advantage to the child she was then expecting; it early proved to be an unusually lively little girl, with the mother's fair face in the bud. The temptation again came over these two lonely people to cling to their child with hope and joy; but the fateful two years had not yet come, and when it did arrive, it seemed to them as if they had merely gained a respite. They dared not yield to their feelings.

The two old people had held themselves much aloof. For the mood that controlled the others could be approached neither with words of consolation nor with the joys of others. Knut was, moreover, too fond of worldly pleasure to remain long in a house of mourning or to be forever taking part in devotional exercises. So he moved over to a small farm which he owned, and which he hitherto had rented; now he took it himself and put it in such fine, tasteful order for his dear Astrid that she, who would greatly have preferred being at Tingvold, remained where *he* was, and laughed with him instead of weeping with their children.

One day when Astrid went over to visit her daughter-in-law, she saw little Mildred, and she observed that the child was left entirely to herself; the mother scarcely ventured to touch her. Moreover, the grandmother noticed that when the father came in, he manifested the same sorrowful reserve toward his only child. Astrid concealed her thoughts, but when she got home to her own dear Knut, she represented to him what a wretched state of affairs there was at Tingvold; *there* was now their place. Little Mildred ought to have some one who was not afraid to take pleasure in her; for there was growing up something very fine and fair for the family in this child. Knut was impressed by his wife's eager zeal, and both the old people packed up and went home.

Mildred thus became the special care of the grandparents, and the old people taught the parents to love the child. But when Mildred was five years old there was born to the house another daughter, who was named Beret, and the result was that Mildred passed most of her time with the old people.

Now the frightened parents once more began to dare believe in life! To this the change in the atmosphere about them contributed not a little. After the loss of the second child people always noticed that they had wept, but never saw them in tears; their sorrow was very unobtrusive.

The peaceful, pious life at Tingvold, bound the servants to the place; and many words of praise of the master and mistress were spoken abroad. They became sensible of this themselves. Both relatives and friends began to seek them out and continued to do so, even though the Tingvold family made no return.

But at church they had not been since their wedding-day. They partook of the sacrament at home, and conducted their own devotional services. But when the second girl was born they felt a desire to be her sponsors themselves, so for the first time they ventured to church. Upon this occasion they visited together the graves of their children, and they walked past Ole Haugen's resting-place without a word or a gesture, and all the people showed them respect. Nevertheless, they continued to live to themselves, and a pious hush lay over the whole gard.

Here one day, at her grandmother's house, little Mildred sang the bridal march. In great alarm old Astrid stopped her work and asked the child where in all the world she had learned this tune. Mildred replied that she had learned it of her.

Old Knut who was sitting there had a good laugh at this, for he knew very well that Astrid had a habit of humming it when she had any work that kept her sitting still. But now little Mildred was begged by both grandpar ents not to sing the tune when her parents could hear. A child is very apt to ask "why?" But when Mildred did so, she received no reply. After this the little girl heard the new herd-boy singing the tune one evening while he was chopping wood. She told this to her grandmother who had also heard it; but Astrid only remarked: "Ah, he will never grow old here!" and sure enough, the next day the boy was sent away. There was no reason given him; he simply was paid his wages and dismissed. Now Mildred became so excited that her grandmother had to endeavor to tell her the history of the bridal march. The little eight-years old girl understood it pretty well, and what she did not understand then became clear to her later. The story exercised on her childhood an influence which nothing else ever did or could produce: it laid the foundation for her future relations to her parents.

Children have an astonishingly early perception of and sympathy for those who are unhappy. Mildred felt that in the presence of her parents all should be still. This was not difficult to put into practice; for they were so gentle and talked to her so incessantly about the kind heavenly Friend of little children, that the room glowed with a magic light. But the story of the bridal march gave her a touching comprehension of what they had passed through. Painful memories she carefully avoided, and manifested a heartfelt affection in all that she dared share with them, and this was their piety, their truthfulness, their quiet ways, their industry. As Beret grew up, she gradually learned to do the same; for woman's vocation as an educator is awakened from childhood up.

In the society of the grandparents the spirits that in the family home were under restraint flowed freely. Here there was singing and dancing; games were played and nursery tales told. And thus the sisters, as they were growing up, divided their time between deep devotion to their melancholy parents in the quiet family sitting-room, and the merry life in the home of their grandparents; but it was so gently divided that it was their parents who besought them to go enjoy themselves with the old people; and the old people who entreated them go back to their parents and "be right good girls."

When a girl of from twelve to sixteen years of age takes into her full confidence a sister of from seven to eleven, she gains as a reward an unbounded devotion. But the younger one is apt to become a little too matured thereby.

Mildred herself, on the other hand, was the gainer in becoming forbearing, compassionate, sympathetic, affable, and she became a source of silent joy to both parents and grandparents.

There is nothing further to narrate until Mildred entered her fifteenth year; then old Knut died, suddenly and easily. Scarcely a moment passed from the time he sat jesting in his home until he lay there a corpse.

The pleasantest thing the grandmother knew after his death was to have Mildred on the little cricket at her feet, where she had been in the habit of having her sit from the time Mildred was small, and either herself to tell the child about Knut, or to have Mildred sing, with a low tra-la-la, the bridal march. In *its* tones Astrid saw Knut's vigorous, dark head emerge from her childhood; in listening to it she could follow him over the grassy slopes of the gard, where as a herd-boy he used to blow his horn, in it she drove to church at his side; in it his merry, clever image most distinctly rose up before her. But in Mildred's soul there began to stir new emotions. While she sat singing to her grandmother, she asked herself: "Will this bridal march ever be played for me?"

From the moment this question presented itself to her, it grew; the march became all aglow with a calm, peaceful happiness. She saw a bridal crown glittering in its sunshine, which opened out a long, bright future for her to ride forward in. She reached the age of sixteen, and she asked herself: "Shall I — ah! shall I ever drive after it myself, followed by father and mother, past a crowd of people who do not laugh, alight with a joyous heart where mother wept, walk past Ole Haugen's grave, and up to the altar in such radiant bliss that father and mother shall have amends for all that they have suffered?"

This was the first train of thought she did not confide to Beret. As time wore on there came to be others. Beret, who was now in her twelfth year, saw plainly that she was left more to herself than she had been, but did not exactly understand that she was being set aside until another was in possession of her privileges. This was the eighteen-years-old, just betrothed, Inga, their cousin who lived on the neighboring gard. When Beret saw her and Mildred go whispering and laughing across the fields, with their arms entwined about each other, after the wont of young girls, she was ready to fling herself down and weep with jealousy.

Mildred was now preparing for confirmation;

thus she became acquainted with those of her own age, and some of them came on Sundays up to Tingvold. They spent their time out in the fields, or in grandmother's house. Tingvold had indeed hitherto been a closed land of promise to the young people of the parish. Nor did there now come any but those of a certain gentle, quiet nature, for it could not be denied that there was something subdued about Mildred that attracted but few.

In those days there was a great deal of singing going on among the young people. Such things are never accidental; nevertheless they have their seasons, and these seasons again have their leaders. Among the latter, oddly enough, there was once more a member of the Haugen family. Wherever there can be found a people, among whom, however many hundred years past it may have been, almost every man and woman have sought and found in song an expression for their deepest feelings and thoughts, and have been themselves able to make the verses which bore the outpourings of their souls, — there the art can never so entirely die out but that it may still live at some parish merry-making, and can easily be awakened even where it has not been heard for a long time. In this parish there had been made many verses, and much music from time out of mind; it was neither *from* nothing nor *for* nothing that Ole Haugen was born here. And now it was his son's son in whom the musical taste of the family lived. Ole Haugen's son had been so much younger than the daughter who had married into the Tingvold family, that she as a married woman had stood sponsor for him. After many changes of fortune, he had, when quite an old man, become proprietor of his father's freeholder's place up the mountain, and singularly enough he had then married for the first time. Several children were born to him, and among them a son, who was called Hans, and who seemed to have inherited his grandfather's talents, not exactly for fiddling, although he did play, but rather for singing old songs and sometimes composing new ones. His taste for music was largely increased through his knowing so few people, although he lived right in their midst. Moreover, there were, indeed, not many who had seen him. The fact was, his old father had been a huntsman, and before his sons were very large the old man used to sit on the hill-side and teach them to load and take aim. His delight is said to have been exceedingly great when the little fellows could earn the powder and shot they used.

Beyond this he never got. Their mother died a short time after him, so the children were left to take care of themselves, and they did so. The boys went hunting, and the girls managed the place on the mountain. They attracted attention when, once in a while, they made their appearance in the valley, but this was not often, for in the winter there was no path, and they had to be content with the trips about the surrounding neighborhood which must be made to sell and carry to its destination their game; and in the summer they were kept in the mountains with travelers. Their place was the highest one in the parish; it was celebrated for having that pure mountain air which is more successful in healing lung weaknesses and shattered nerves than any known medicine, and so every year it was overrun with people from town or from abroad. The family added several buildings to their place; but still their rooms were filled. From poor, aye, pitiably poor people, these brothers and sisters had thus worked their way up to prosperity. Intercourse with so many strangers had given them a peculiar stamp; they had even learned something of the foreign languages. Several years before Hans had bought the place of his brothers and sisters, so that it stood in his name; he was at this time twenty-eight years old.

None of them had ever set foot in the home of their Tingvold relatives. Endrid and Randi Tingvold had certainly not consciously forbidden this; but they could tolerate the mention of the name Haugen as little as they could the sound of the bridal march. The poor father of these children had upon one occasion been made to feel this, and so Hans forbade his brothers and sisters to go there. But the Tingvold girls, who took so much pleasure in singing, had an incredible desire to know Hans, and felt ashamed that their parents had neglected these relatives. In the recent gatherings of girls at the gard, there were more questions asked and more anecdotes told about Hans and his brothers and sisters than about anything else.

In the midst of this delightful period of song and social intercourse, Mildred was confirmed, at the approach of her seventeenth year. A little while before this all had been quiet about her; a short time after it was the same. But in the spring, or rather in the summer, she was to go up to the sæter with the cattle, as all girls do after they are confirmed. She was exceedingly glad! Her betrothed friend Inga was to be at the neighboring sæter.

Beret was to be allowed to accompany her

sister to the sæter, and Mildred's longing affected her also. But when they got up to the sæter, where Beret became completely absorbed in all the unaccustomed surroundings, Mildred continued to be as restless as before; she went about her work with the cattle and the dairy in an absent-minded manner; but the long weary time that still remained hung heavily on her hands. For hours together she would sit with Inga, listening while she talked of her lover, then would not go near her for days. If Inga came to see her, she was pleased and affectionate, and acted as though she repented her faithlessness, but she soon grew tired of her again. She seldom had anything to say to Beret, and often when Beret addressed her the child got no other answers than Yes and No. Beret went weeping after the cattle and joined the herd-boys. Mildred felt that there was something in all this that had been broken to pieces; but with the best will she knew not how to mend it.

With such thoughts as these, she was one day sitting in the vicinity of the sæter green. Some goats had found their opportunity to straggle away from the flock, and she had to watch them. It was in the forenoon of a warm day; she sat in the shade of a ridge overgrown with young trees and birch; she had thrown off her jacket and taken out her knitting. She was expecting Inga. She heard a rustling behind her. "There she comes," thought she, and looked up.

But a louder noise followed than it seemed to her Inga could make; the bushes crackled and creaked under a heavy tread; Mildred grew pale and started up, and saw a rim of fur and a pair of blinking eyes underneath; it must be a bear's head! She felt a desire to scream, but could not find voice; she wanted to spring up, but could not stir. Then the object that had startled her was drawn up full length before her; it proved to be a tall, broad-shouldered man, with a fur cap and a gun in his hand. He paused suddenly among the young trees and looked at her. His eyes were keen, but in constant motion; he made a few steps forward, then with a bound stood on the greensward at her side. Something brushed against her knee; she gave a low scream. It was his dog, whom she had not seen before.

"Ugh!" cried she. "I almost thought it was a bear that was trampling down the young trees, that is the reason why I was so frightened."

She tried to laugh.

"Ah, you were not far from the truth!" said

he, and he spoke with extraordinary gentleness. "Kvas and I were just on the track of a bear, but we have lost it; and if there be any wraith [1] accompanying *me*, it is certainly a bear."

He smiled. She stared at him. What sort of a person was this? Tall, broad-shouldered, with eyes that were constantly changing, so that she could not look into them; and thus he stood close beside her as if he had sprung out of the earth, with his gun and his dog. She felt a strong impulse to say: "Go away from me!" but instead she herself drew back a few paces, and asked: "Who are you?" for she was actually afraid.

"Hans Haugen," he replied absently; for his attention had been called to the dog, that had evidently found the scent again. He turned hastily toward her to say farewell; but when he looked at her he saw the young girl standing before him, with the hot blood gushing up in streams over cheeks, neck, and throat.

"What is the matter!" cried he, astonished.

She knew not what to do, whether she should run away, turn round, or sit down.

"Who are you? asked he.

At once she was again bathed in blushes

[1] The old superstition, that every man has his wraith (vardöger in his train (an invisible animal, which is an expression of his nature), is still common among the peasants. — TRANSLATOR.

for to tell him her name would be to explain all she had in thought in regard to him.

"*Who are you?*" he asked once more,—which was the most natural question in the world, and certainly deserved an answer; nor could she refuse one; she felt ashamed of herself and ashamed of her parents that they could have neglected their own kinsfolk; but the name must be spoken.

"Mildred Tingvold," she whispered, and burst into tears.

Aye, to be sure; none of the Tingvold family had he ever before of his own free will addressed. But what had now occurred was different from anything he had imagined; he fixed a pair of large eyes on her. There flitted through his memory the story about her mother's weeping like this in church on her wedding-day; perhaps it runs in the family, thought he, and felt a desire to get away from it.

"You must excuse me, if I have alarmed you," said he, and followed the dog; it was already bounding over the ridge.

When she ventured to raise her eyes, he had just neared the crest, and he turned and looked at her. It was but for a moment, for just then the dog barked on the other side; it startled him, he raised his gun and was off. Mildred remained motionless with her eyes fixed on the spot where he had stood, when a shot alarmed her. Could it be the bear? Could it have been so near her? And off she scrambled where *he* but now had climbed, and stood where he had stood, shading her eyes with her hand from the sun, and sure enough, half hidden by some brushwood, he was stooping over a large bear! Before she was aware of it she had sprung down to him; he beamed a smile on her, and he told her, speaking in a low, flexible voice, how it had all come to pass, that they had lost the scent, afterwards, though, found it here; he explained why the dog had been unable to scent the bear before he came close to his track; and amid this she had forgotten her tears and bashfulness, and he had drawn his knife. He wanted to skin the animal at once. The flesh was not worth anything at this time of year, he would bury it without delay; but the skin he wanted to take with him. And he requested her to help him, and before she knew what she was doing, she was holding while he was flaying; afterward she ran down to the sæter for an axe and a spade, and although she was afraid of the bear, and although it smelled vilely, she continued to help him until he was through. By this time it was past noon.

and he invited himself to dine with her. He washed both himself and the hide, which was no easy task, and when he got through he sat down beside her in the sheeling; for *she*, to her shame, had not the dinner yet ready. He chatted away about one thing and another, easily and pleasantly, but in a very low tone, such as people are apt to use who have been much alone. Mildred gave the shortest answers she could; but when she sat right opposite him at the table, she could neither speak nor eat, so that they often sat in silence. When he had finished, he turned on his stool, and filled and lighted a short pipe. He, too, had become rather more taciturn than he had been, and presently he rose.

"I have a long walk home," said he, and as he gave her his hand, he added in still lower tones: "Do you sit every day where I found you to-day?"

He held her hand a moment as though awaiting an answer. She dared not look up, much less reply. Then she felt a hasty pressure of her hand. "Thank you for the day!" he said softly, and before she could gain command of herself, she saw him with the bear-skin over his shoulders, gun in hand, dog at his side, walking over the heather. She saw him outlined against the sky, as he reached the summit of the mountains; his light, brisk step bore him swiftly away; she stepped outside of the door and watched him until he had disappeared from view.

Now for the first time she perceived that her heart was throbbing so violently that she had to press her hands over it. A little while later she lay on the greensward with her face on her arm, and most accurately passed in review the occurrences of the day. She saw him emerge from among the young trees above where she sat; she saw him, with his broad shoulders and restless eyes, standing right in front of her; she felt the advantage he had over her, and her own alarm, and her disgraceful tears; she saw him on the crest of the ridge against the sun; she heard the shot, she was on her knees in front of him while he was skinning the bear; she heard over again every word he had uttered, and his low voice, which had so friendly a sound that it thrilled her through and through as she thought of it; she heard it again from the stool in front of the hearth, while she was cooking, and from the table while she was eating; she felt how she then no longer dared look him in the eyes, and she felt that she finally had embarrassed him too, for he had grown silent

She heard him speak once again, as he took her hand, and she felt his grasp, — it thrilled her still from head to foot! She saw him crossing the heather, walking on and on! Would he ever come again? After the way she had conducted herself — impossible! Ah, how strong, beautiful, self-reliant was not all that she had seen of him, and how stupid and miserable was not all that he had seen of her! Yes, miserable, from her first scream at the dog to her blush of shame and her tears; from the clumsy assistance she gave him to the meal she was so long in getting ready for him! And to think she could not answer No, not even when he looked at her; and then, at last, when he asked if she sat every day at the foot of the ridge, that she did not say No, for she did not sit there every day! Did not her silence seem as if she were begging him, mutely imploring him to come and see? The whole of her pitiable helplessness — might it not be misconstrued in the same way? Ah, how mortified she was! There tingled a burning sense of shame through her whole body, especially in her face, as she buried it deeper and deeper; and then she conjured up the whole scene again, his magnificence and her wretchedness, whereupon her mortification increased.

When the bells announced the approach of the cattle she was still lying there, but now made haste to get ready for them. Beret, who came too, saw at once that there was something amiss; for Mildred addressed to her the most absurd questions and answers, and acted so stupidly that Beret several times stood still and stared at her! And when it was time for supper, and Mildred said that she could not eat, and instead of taking her seat at the table, sat down outside of the door, nothing was lacking to make Beret the exact picture of a hunting dog on the scent, but to have her ears point forward. Beret ate her supper and undressed — she and her sister slept in the same bed — and when Mildred did not join her she rose up softly many times and looked to see if her sister were still sitting at the door, and if she were alone. Yes, she sat there, and always alone. The clock struck eleven, then twelve, then one, and Mildred still sat outside, and Beret did not sleep. She pretended to be asleep, to be sure, when Mildred finally came, and Mildred moved very, very quietly; but after she got into bed Beret heard her sigh, she heard her say her customary evening prayer, so mournfully, heard her whisper: "Oh, help me in this, dear, dear God!"

"What does she want God to help her about?" thought Beret. She could not sleep; she heard her sister, too, vainly trying to arrange herself for sleep, now on one, now on the other side; she saw her at last give up entirely, push away the cover, and putting her hands under her head lie there staring before her, with wide open eyes. More she neither saw nor heard, for now she fell asleep. When she awoke the next morning, her sister was no longer in bed. Beret sprang up; the sun was already high in the heavens, the cattle had long been astir. She found her breakfast set aside, made haste to eat, then went out and found Mildred at work; but she was looking very haggard. Beret told her that she would at once find the cattle and go with them. The other made no reply, but she gave Beret a look that seemed to be intended to express her thanks. Beret pondered a few moments and then left.

Mildred looked around; yes, she was entirely alone. Then she made haste to get her milk vessels in order, the rest might be attended to as best it could. She washed herself, and brushed her hair, and then hastened into the sheeling to change her clothes, took her knitting and went toward the ridge.

She had none of the new strength of tne new day, for she had scarcely slept at all, and had eaten almost nothing for twenty-four hours. She walked as one in a dream, and it seemed as if she could not grasp a single clear idea until she reached the spot where she had been sitting on the previous day.

But she had no sooner taken her seat there than she thought: "If he should come and find me here, he must of course believe?"— Involuntarily she started up. Then she saw his dog on the ridge; it stood still a moment watching her, then came springing down toward her, wagging its tail. Every drop of blood in her body stood still. There! There he stood, with his gun, in the sun, just as the day before; he had come another way to-day! He smiled at her, hesitated a little, then climbed over the edge of the ridge and soon stood in front of her. She had given a little scream, and then had sunk into her seat. It was utterly impossible for her to rise again, her knitting fell from her hands, she turned her face away. He did not speak. But she heard him throw himself down on the grass just in front of her, with his eyes fixed on hers, and she saw the dog on the other side with its eyes resting on him. She felt that although she sat with her face averted, he could see it, could see her blushes. His hurried breathing quickened hers; she thought she felt his breath on her hand, but she dared not stir. She did not wish him to speak, and yet his silence was terrible. She could not help understanding why he sat there, and greater shame than that which overpowered her had never before been felt. But it was not right in him to come, and still worse was it for him to *be sitting here*. Then one of her hands was seized, and held tight, then the other; she *had* to turn a little at this, and with his kind, strong eyes and hand he drew her gently to him. She glided down on the grass at his side, so that her head fell on his shoulder. She felt him stroking her hair with one hand; but she dared not look up. Her whole conduct was supremely unbecoming, and so she burst into a violent fit of weeping.

"Aye, if you weep, I will laugh," said he; "for what has happened to us two is something both to laugh and cry over!"

But his voice quivered. And now he whispered into her ear that yesterday when he left her, he kept drawing continually nearer and nearer to her. This had increased to such a degree that when he reached his mountain hut he could do nothing but let the German, his associate, shift for himself, while he pushed on alone up the mountains. He had passed the night partly sitting, partly walking about on the heights; in the morning he had gone home to breakfast, but started off again forthwith. He was twenty-eight years old, and no small boy; but this he knew, that either the girl must be his or all would be lost. He wandered to the place where he had met her the day before, he did *not* expect to find her, he only thought he would sit down here by himself a while. When he saw her, he was at first startled, but then he thought that her feelings must be the same as his, and so he resolved at once to put her to the test, and when he saw that she really felt as he did, why then — yes, then — and he raised her head and she no longer wept, and his eyes glowed with such strange brilliancy that she was forced to gaze into them, and she blushed and bowed her head. But he went on talking, in his low, pleasant voice.

The sun shone on the tops of the trees that covered the slope, the birches quivered in a gentle breeze, the chattering of the birds blended with the babbling of a little brook that flowed over a stony bottom close by. Neither took note of the time that passed as they sat there together, it was the dog that first roused them. It had made several excursions around, stretching itself out in its place again after each one; but now it sprang barking down the hill. Both started up, stood a while and listened. But nothing could be seen. They looked again at each other, and then he took her up on his arm. She had never been carried since she was a child, and there was something in the act that made her utterly helpless. He was her defense, her future, her everlasting happiness, she must heed her instincts. Not a word was spoken. He held her, she clung to him. He bore her to the spot where she had first been sitting; there he seated himself and cautiously put her down at his side. She bowed her head lower than ever, that she might not be seen by him now that she had been thus dealt with. He was just about to turn to her when a voice right in front of them, called out, in tones of utter astonishment: " Mildred ! "

It was Inga, who had followed in the track of the dog. Mildred sprang up; she gazed at her friend for an instant, then ran to her, put one arm about her neck and laid her head on her shoulder.

" Who is he ? " whispered Inga, drawing her arm around her, and Mildred felt how she trembled.

But Mildred did not stir. Inga knew very well who he was, for she was acquainted with him; but she could not believe her own eyes! Then Hans drew nearer.

"I thought you knew me," said he calmly; "I am Hans Haugen."

At the sound of his voice, Mildred raised her head. He held out his hand; she walked up to him and took it, and looked at Inga with shame and joy blended in blushing confusion.

Hans took his gun and said farewell, whispering to Mildred as he did so, —

"You may be sure I will come soon again after this!"

Both girls accompanied him down to the dairy, and saw him walk away in the direction he had taken the day before. They watched him until he had disappeared from their sight. Mildred stood, leaning on Inga, and the latter felt that her friend could neither stir nor speak. But when Hans was quite out of sight, Mildred's head drooped on Inga's shoulder, and she said, —

"Ask me no questions, for I cannot tell you anything."

For a time she continued to nestle up against Inga, and then they went to the sheeling There Mildred remembered that she had left everything in disorder behind her, and Inga now helped her. During their work they did not say much to each other; at all events, not about anything else than the work.

Mildred brought forward the noon-day repast, but could eat very little herself, although she felt the need of both food and sleep. Inga left her as soon as she could; she saw that Mildred preferred to be alone.

When Inga was gone, Mildred laid herself down on the bed and tried to sleep. Just once more, though, she wanted to single out from the day's occurrences something that he had said and that seemed to her the most delightful of all. In so doing she had occasion to ask herself what reply she had made to this. And then it became clear to her that she had not said one word — indeed, through their entire interview not a single word! She rose up in bed. He could not have gone many paces alone, before this must have occurred to him also; and what must he then have thought? That she was like one walking about in her sleep, or like a person utterly devoid of will. How could he long continue to be attracted to her. Indeed, it was not until he was away from her, in the first place, that he discovered his love for her; she trembled to think what discoveries he might make this day. Again, as on the preceding day, she sat down outside of the door. Through her whole life Mildred had been accustomed to take care of herself; she had led such a sheltered life. Therefore, in her entire behavior during the past twenty-four hours, she thought she had shown neither discretion nor consideration, scarcely even modesty. She knew nothing of such things, either from books or from real life; she saw with the vision of peasants, and no one has stricter rules of propriety. It is seemly, according to them, to suppress one's emotions; it is modest to be tardy in the expression of one's feelings. She, who beyond all others, had adhered to these rules throughout her whole life, and who, consequently, had enjoyed the esteem of all about her, had in one single day yielded herself entirely to a man she had never before seen! In the course of time he would be the very one who would most despise her! When it was a thing that could not be told, not even to Inga, what must it not be!

When Beret appeared at the first sound of the cattle bells in the distance, she found her sister lying outside of the sheeling, looking like one in whom there was no life. She stood by her until Mildred was compelled to raise her head and look at her. Mildred's eyes were red with weeping, her whole expression that of one who is suffering. But her countenance changed when she caught sight of Beret, for Beret's face showed traces of agitation.

"What is the matter with you?" she exclaimed.

"Nothing!" replied Beret, and remained standing, with her eyes averted from Mildred, so that the latter had to drop hers, turn and rise to prepare for the evening meal.

They did not meet again until supper-time, when they sat facing each other. As Mildred was unable to eat more than a few spoonfuls herself, her eyes now and then wandered absently from one to the other at the table, but they rested chiefly on Beret, who seemed as if she would never get through. She was not eating, she was devouring her food like a hungry dog.

"Have you taken no food before, to-day?" asked Mildred.

"No," answered Beret, and continued eating. Presently Mildred asked, —

"Have you not been with the herd-boys?"

"No," replied both she and the herd-boys.

In their presence Mildred would not ask any more questions, and later her own morbid mind made her quite unfit to take charge of her sister, and, as it seemed to her too, quite unworthy. This thought was but an addition to the growing reproaches, which were throbbing one by one through her soul, as she sat all the evening and into the night in her place outside of the sheeling door.

In the crimson flush of the evening, in the cold gray night, no peace, not the slightest inclination for sleep. The poor child had never before been in trouble. Ah, how she prayed! She would cease and begin again; she used prayers which she knew, and she poured out her soul in words of her own, and finally, totally exhausted, she sought her bed. There she again collected her thoughts; but her strength was all gone; she could only take up the burden of her prayer: "Help me! dear, dear God, oh, help me!"— and she kept repeating this, now in low tones, now aloud; for she was having a struggle within herself as to whether she should give him up or not. Suddenly she was so frightened that she gave a shriek; for quick as lightning Beret had darted up and was kneeling by her.

"Who is he?" she whispered, her large eyes flashing fire, and her heated face and short breath betokening great agitation of mind.

Mildred, overpowered by her self-torture, ex

hausted in soul and body, could make no reply; she had become so alarmed that she felt like sobbing aloud.

"Who is he?" repeated the other, in threatening tones, bringing her face nearer to Mildred's; "it is no use for you to hide it any longer; I was watching you two the whole time to-day!"

Mildred held up her arms, by way of defense, but Beret seized them and drew them down.

"Who is he, I say?"—this time she looked Mildred straight in the eyes.

"Beret, Beret!" wailed the other; ' have I ever shown you anything but kindness since you were a little child? Why are you so unkind to me, now that I am in such distress?"

Beret let go of her arm, for Mildred was shedding tears. But Beret's breath was hot, and her heart throbbed as if it would burst.

"Is it Hans Haugen?" whispered she.

Breathless silence ensued.

"Yes," finally whispered Mildred, and burst into tears.

Then Beret drew down her sister's arm once more;—she wanted to look into her eyes.

"Why did you not tell me this, Mildred?" she asked, with the same burning zeal.

"Beret, indeed I did not know it myself,"

was the reply. "I never saw him in my life until yesterday. And no sooner had I seen him than I gave myself to him; that is just what torments me so that I feel as if I must die!"

"Did you never see him before yesterday?" screamed Beret, in the greatest astonishment.

"Never in my life," replied Mildred, vehemently. "Can you imagine so great a shame, Beret?"

But at this Beret flung herself over her, threw her arms about her neck, and kissed her over and over again.

"Dear, sweet Mildred, how delightful it is!" she whispered, all sparkling with delight. "Ah, how delightful it is!" she repeated, and kissed her. "And how I will keep the secret, Mildred!"—and she gave her sister a squeeze, then started up again. "And to think you believed I could not keep it to myself!" and she fell into sudden distress. "*I* not keep a secret when it concerned you, Mildred!" she began to cry. "Why have you forgotten me of late? Why have you put Inga in my place? Oh, what sorrow you have caused me! When you knew how fond I was of you, Mildred!" and she hid her face in her sister's bosom.

But Mildred now drew her arm round her and kissed her, and then assured her that she had not thought of this until now, and that she would never push her aside again, and that henceforth she would place implicit confidence in her, she was so good and true; — and she patted her, and Beret patted her in return. Beret rose up again on her knee; she wanted to see her sister's eyes in the glow of the summer night, which was already beginning to be tinged with the rosy flush of morning.

"Mildred, how handsome he is!" was Beret's first exultant shout. "How did he come? How did you first see him? What did he say? How did it happen?"

And what Mildred a few hours before believed she could never tell any one, she now found herself freely recounting to her sister; she was interrupted now and then by having Beret fling herself over her and give her a hug; but this only increased Mildred's delight in telling her story. They laughed and they wept; sleep had entirely escaped their minds. The sun found them thus: the one lying down, or resting on her elbow, transported by her own story; the other on her knees in front of her, with half parted lips, glittering eyes, and now and then flinging herself over her sister, in an exuberance of delight.

They rose together, and did their work together; and when they were through with it, and just for the sake of appearances had eaten their breakfast, they both dressed for the interview. He must surely come soon! The girls sat down in their holiday attire at the foot of the ridge, and Beret showed Mildred where *she* had been lying the day before; the dog had often come there to her. One sister's story followed swiftly upon that of the other; the weather too was fine to-day, only a few clouds were visible. They had soon chatted away the time beyond the hour when Hans was expected; but they continued to talk, and forgot it only to remember it again, and Beret sprang to her feet several times, and ran up to the crest to see if he were coming; but she neither saw nor heard anything of him. Both girls grew impatient, and Mildred suddenly became so to such a degree that Beret was alarmed. She represented to her sister that he was really not his own master; for two days the German had been left to fish and shoot and prepare his meals alone; that would scarcely answer three days in succession; and Mildred found that there was some justice in this.

"What do you think father and mother will say to this?" asked Beret, merely to divert her sister's thoughts.

But the moment she had uttered the words, she regretted having done so. Mildred grew pale and stared at Beret, who stared at her in return. Had Mildred never thought of this before? Yes, to be sure she had; but as one thinks of something far away. Fear at what Hans Haugen might think of her, shame at her own weakness and stupidity, had so completely absorbed her that she had thrust all else aside. Now the case was reversed; her parents suddenly and wholly occupied her thoughts!

Beret again strove to console her. When they saw him they would justify Mildred in what she had done; nor would they make *her* unhappy, who had been their joy; grandmother would help her too; no one could have any fault to find with Hans Haugen, and *he* would never give up!

All this rushed past Mildred, but she was thinking of something else, and in order to gain time to consider properly, she begged Beret to get the dinner ready. Beret walked slowly away, glancing over her shoulder several times.

Now what Mildred was pondering upon was: "Shall I tell father and mother about this at once?" Excited as she was from the tremendous strain of the day, the question grew to the size of a mountain. It seemed to her that she would be committing a sin if she received him now. She ought not to have engaged herself without her parents' consent; but she had been powerless to do otherwise. Now that it was done her only course was to seek her parents without delay! She rose to her feet, a light dawned in her soul. What was right must be done. When Hans appeared here again, she must have spoken to her parents. "Is not that so?" she queried, yet not exactly as a question; and "Yes!" she seemed to hear some one reply, although no one had spoken. She hastened to the dairy to tell Beret of this. But Beret was neither in the sheeling, nor in the dairy.

"Beret!" she called. "Beret! Beret!"

The echo repeated the name from every side; but it gave her no Beret. Round about she went searching for her sister without finding her. She had been agitated before, she was terrified now. Beret's wide-opened eyes, and the question: "What do you think father and mother will say to this?" kept growing larger and larger.

Could Beret have possibly gone to them herself? It would be just like her! Vehement as the child was, she would want to have the question decided, and Mildred consoled forthwith. Most assuredly she had gone!

But if Beret should be the first to carry this to her parents, they would misunderstand it; and Mildred struck briskly into the path leading to the parish! Once on the way she walked faster and faster, borne onward by ever-increasing excitement. She was not aware of this, only there was a buzzing in her head, a pressure about the heart, — she panted for breath. She was forced to sit down and rest awhile. But she could get no rest sitting, she must lie on the ground. She flung herself down on her arm, and thus she fell asleep.

For two days and nights she had scarcely slept or eaten, and what power this would naturally have over the soul and body of a child who had hitherto calmly and regularly taken her meals and slept in her father's house, she did not understand.

Now Beret had not gone to their parents but had started off after Hans Haugen! She had a long distance to go, and part of the way lay through an unknown region, along the edge of a wood, and later she had to go farther up the mountains, across plateaus that were not quite secure from wild beasts, which had been showing themselves about here of late. But she went bravely onward, for Hans must come, or it would be hard for Mildred: she scarcely knew her sister as she appeared now!

She was light-hearted and gay, her sister's adventure went tripping along with her. Hans Haugen was the most distinguished person she knew in this world, and Mildred deserved the most distinguished! It was no wonder that Mildred gave herself at once to him, no more than it was strange that he fell in love with Mildred at first sight. If their parents could not understand this they would have to do as they pleased, and these two must brave resistance as her great grandfather and her grand father had done; — and she began to sing the bridal march of her family. It rang jubilantly out over the desert wastes and died away in the hazy atmosphere.

On the top of the mountain she paused and shouted hurrah! But a strip of the extreme and uppermost part of the parish was visible from where she stood; bordering on it she saw the last edge of the wood, beyond it the heath, and here where she was standing nothing but stones and rocky plains in rigid undulations. She sped swiftly onward in the buoyant air. She knew that the mountain hut must be situated in a direct line with yonder snow-capped mountain, whose peak towered above all the others, and pretty soon she was convinced that she had not very far to go. In order to make sure of her course she climbed upon a large loose stone, and then saw a mountain lake just below her. Whether it was a hut or a rock that she now saw beside the lake, she could not decide, for sometimes it seemed to resemble a hut, sometimes a rock. But close by a mountain lake his hut was said to stand. Yes, indeed, it was unquestionably by this very one, for there was a boat rounding yonder point! Two men sat in it; this must be he and the German. Down she sprang and started forward. But what she had thought so near, proved to be far away, and she ran and ran. The anticipation of meeting Hans Haugen excited her.

Hans Haugen sat secure in his boat with the German, unconscious of all the commotion he had caused. Hans had never been frightened himself. He was only happy, and he sat there making some verses for the bridal march.

He was no great poet; but he had put together something about their ride to church, and their meeting in the woods served for the refrain of each stanza. He was whistling and fishing and enjoying himself extremely; the German was busy fishing and left him in peace.

They now heard shouting on the shore; both Hans and the bearded German raised their eyes and saw a young girl beckoning to them. They conferred together a moment, and then rowed to shore. Here Hans sprang out and moored the boat, and both men loaded themselves with the guns, coats, fish, and fishing tackle; but while the German went straight to the hut, Hans, with his burden, walked up to Beret, who was standing on a stone near by.

"Who are you?" asked he.

"Beret, Mildred's sister," said she.

He flushed crimson, and she did the same. But presently he grew pale.

"Is anything the matter?" cried he.

"No, nothing, except that you must come. She cannot bear to be alone now."

He stood still a moment gravely contemplating her. Then he turned and went toward the hut. The German had paused outside to hang up the fishing tackle; Hans now did the same, while the two exchanged some words. Inside of the hut, ever since Beret shouted, two dogs had been barking with all their might and main. The men went in together; but as they opened the door the dogs rushed out, Hans's and the German's, but were at once sternly recalled. All became still, and it was a long time before Hans came out again. But when he did appear, he wore other clothes than before, and he had his gun and his dog with him. The German accompanied him out. And they took each other by the hand, as though they were saying farewell for a long time. Hans at once approached Beret.

"Can you walk fast?" asked he.

"Yes, to be sure I can."

And he walked and she ran; the dog bounded along in front of them.

As it had not occurred to him that Mildred could feel less secure and happy over their betrothal than he himself had felt, this summons came to him as a message from a new world of thought. Of course, she was anxious about her parents! She was alarmed, too, at the haste in which everything had been brought to pass — to be sure she was! He understood this so well now that he was thoroughly astonished at himself for not having understood it before — and he walked on! Why, even on him the meeting with Mildred had made an overwhelming impression; what must not she, a child, quiet and retired as the home of her parents, experience at being cast out in a storm? And he strode on!

During this rapid march Beret had skipped

along at his side, keeping her face, as far as possible, turned toward his. She had now and then caught a glimpse of his large eyes and flushed cheeks; but he was so completely encircled by his thoughts, that he had not seen her distinctly, and at last he lost sight of her altogether. He turned; she was a considerable distance behind him; but she was straining every nerve to keep up. She had been too proud to say that she could not endure such a march. But when he paused and waited until she came up, all out of breath, the tears started to her eyes.

"Ah! Am I walking too fast?" and he held out his hand as he spoke.

She was panting so that she could not answer.

"Let us sit down a little while," said he, and drew her toward him. "Come!" and he pulled her down into a seat at his side.

She grew rosier, if possible, than before; and she did not look at him. She was gasping as if she were losing her breath.

"I am so thirsty," was the first thing she could say.

They rose again, and he looked round; but there was no water near at hand.

"We must wait till we get on farther; then

we will find a brook," said he; "it would not be good for you to drink just now, either."

He sat down again and she took her seat on the stone in front of him.

"I *ran* all the way coming here," said she, by way of apology. "And I did not eat any dinner," she added presently; nor did I sleep any last night," she further volunteered.

Instead of expressing sympathy for her, he asked, hurriedly, —

"Then, I suppose, Mildred, too, ate no dinner, and, perhaps, did not sleep last night?"

"Why, Mildred did not sleep any the night before either, and she has not eaten, so far as I have noticed, no, not for " — she considered a while — " for ever so long."

He started up.

"Can you go on now?"

"Yes, I think I can."

And he took her by the hand, and the hurried tramp began anew. After a little while he saw that she could not continue at this rate, so he took off his jacket, gave it to her, and picking her up carried her. This she would not permit on any account. But he bore her lightly onward, and Beret held fast to his waistcoat-band; him she dared not touch. Presently she told him that now she was rested and could run very well. He put her down, took his jacket himself and hung it across his gun, and pushed on. When the brook was reached, they paused and rested a little before she drank. When she rose, he looked at her and smiled.

"You are a nice little girl," said he.

Evening was drawing near when they reached their journey's end. Mildred was sought in vain both in the dairy and on the ridge; their shouts died away in the distance and both were becoming alarmed, when Hans noticed that the dog was sniffing at something. They ran forward; it was Mildred's kerchief. Hans immediately gave a sign to the dog to seek the owner of the kerchief, and off the animal went! They followed over the mountain toward the other side, that is, in the direction toward the Tingvold region. Could she have gone home?

Beret told about her thoughtless question and its results, and Hans replied that he could well imagine that it would be so. Beret began to cry. Should they go after her or not? Beret chimed in: "Yes, yes!" she was quite distracted. Before starting they must go to the neighboring sæter to ask some one to look after the cattle. While they were still discussing this, all the time following the dog, they saw it pause and look back, wagging its tail. They ran forward and there they found Mildred!

She was lying on her arm, with her face half buried in the heather. They approached with soft steps, the dog licked her hand and cheek; she wiped the spots it had touched and changed her position, but slept on.

"Let her sleep!" whispered Hans; "and you go and meet the cattle; I hear the bells."

After Beret had started, he hastened after her.

"Bring some food with you when you come back," whispered he.

Now he seated himself at a short distance from Mildred, drew the dog to him, forced it to lie down, and sat there holding it, to prevent it from barking if a bird or some stray animal should stir near them.

The evening was cloudy; there was a gray light over the ridges and plateaus; all around was hushed; not so much as a little bird broke the stillness of the air. He sat or rather reclined with his hand on the dog. What should be agreed upon when Mildred awoke, he had quickly settled in his own mind. The future was without a cloud: he lay there gazing up at the sky, undisturbed by a shadow of anxiety.

He knew that their meeting was a miracle God himself had told them they must walk through life together!

He busied himself once more with the bridal march; a suppressed joy reigned within his soul, he imprisoned his thoughts therein.

It must have been after eight o'clock when Beret came back, bringing food with her. Mildred was not yet awake. Beret put down her load, stood watching them a while, then seated herself, but at some distance from the others. They waited fully an hour more, during which Beret often jumped up to keep herself from falling asleep. Toward ten o'clock Mildred awoke. She turned several times, opened her eyes at last, saw where she was lying, sat up, looked at the others. She was half intoxicated with sleep, which kept her from clearly comprehending where she was and what she saw, till Hans rose, and smiling, approached her. Then she held out both hands towards him.

He sat down at her side.

"Now you have slept, Mildred."

"Yes, now I have slept."

"Now you are hungry."

"Yes, I am hungry." Here Beret drew near with the food.

Mildred looked at it and at them. "Have slept long?" said she.

"Yes, you have. It must be nine o'clock. Look at the sun!"

Now for the first time she seemed to recall all that had occurred.

"Have you been here long?"

"Oh — no; but eat now!"

She began.

"You were on your way down to the valley?" inquired Hans, drawing his face nearer to hers.

She blushed.

"Yes," whispered she.

"To-morrow, when you have had your sleep *quite* out, we two will go down there together."

Her eyes were fastened on his; first wide-open and wondering, then smiling, filled with gratitude; but she said nothing. After this she seemed to revive. She asked Beret where *she* had been, and Beret told her she had gone in search of Hans, — and he told the rest. Mildred ate and listened, and it was evident that the old enchantment was gradually stealing over her again. She laughed merrily at hearing that the dog had found her and licked her face without waking her. The dog was sitting by, greedily watching every morsel she ate; now she began to share her meal with it.

As soon as she had finished, they went slowly

toward the sæter, and not long after Beret was in bed. The two others sat down outside of the door. There began to fall a drizzling rain, but as the roof projected they did not heed it. The fog closed about the dairy; they sat as within a magic circle. The atmosphere was, consequently, more dark than light. Subdued words fell from their lips, each one bringing confidence. For the first time they could talk together. He tenderly begged her pardon for not having remembered that she might be differently constituted than he, and that she had parents to consult. She acknowledged her fright, and said that from the moment she had met him she had ceased to be herself; indeed, she had even forgotten her parents. She no doubt had more to say, yet she would not continue. But in their trembling joy, everything spoke, even to the softest breath. The first delicate outpouring of soul to soul, which with others usually precedes and prepares the way for the first embrace, with these two followed it. The first true questions stole through the twilight, the first true answers floated back. Light as a breath, soft as down, the words fell on the air, and in the same way were wafted back. Thus it was that Mildred at last found the courage, softly, hesitatingly, to ask if he had not considered her conduct very strange. He assured her that it had not seemed so to him, no, not once. Had he not noticed that she had been silent throughout the entire interview yesterday? No, he had not observed it. Had he not thought— For a long time she failed to find words, but they came finally in a low whisper, and with averted face, — that she was very hasty in yielding to him? No, he had only thought how delightfully the whole thing had come to pass. But what did he think of her for crying, the first time he saw her? Well, he had not comprehended it then, but now he understood it very well, and he was glad that she was just as she was.

All these answers made her so happy that she longed to be alone. And as he had divined this too, he rose softly and bade her go to bed. She got up also. He nodded and went slowly to the stable, where he was to sleep; but she hastened into the sheeling, undressed herself, and not until she was in bed did she clasp her hands and thank God. Oh, how she thanked Him! She thanked Him for Hans, for his love, his forbearance, his charming nature; she could not find words for all she wanted to say; so she thanked God for all, all, everything, even for the pain of these two days; for how great had it not made her joy. She gave thanks for the solitude of the mountain, and prayed God to accompany her from these lofty heights down to her parents, then turned her thoughts again to Hans, and gave thanks for him, fervent thanks.

When she came out in the morning — Beret still slept — Hans was standing in the yard. The dog had had a whipping: it had disturbed a ptarmigan, and was now lying at its master's feet trying to curry favor with him. When Hans saw Mildred he released the dog; the delighted animal sprang up on him and on her, it barked a good-morning greeting, wagged its tail, and was the living expression of their bright, young happiness. Hans helped Mildred and the boys with the morning work, and when at last they sat down to breakfast, Beret too had risen. Every time Hans glanced at Beret she blushed, and when Mildred, after they had left the table, took hold of his watch-chain while she was talking with him, Beret hastened from the room. She was hard to find when they were ready to go.

"Listen, Mildred," said Hans, after they had gone a short distance, coming nearer to her and walking softly: " I have been thinking of something I did not find an opportunity to say to you yesterday."

His voice sounded so solemn that she raised her eyes to his face. He spoke slowly, and without looking at her.

"I wanted to ask you — if it is the will of God that we should be united — to come home to my house after the wedding."

She grew red, and after a while answered evasively, —

"What would father and mother say to that?"

He walked on for some time before he replied, —

"I did not suppose it would matter much to them if we two were agreed."

It was the first time his words had wounded her. She made no rejoinder. He seemed to be waiting for her to speak, and finally added more softly, —

"It is my wish that we two should be alone — that we might become used to each other."

Now she began to understand him better; but she could not yet find words. He walked on as before, slowly and without looking at her; he, too, was silent now. She felt oppressed and gave him a searching look. She saw that he was very pale.

"But, Hans!" she exclaimed, and paused, without being herself aware of it.

Hans also stood still, glanced hastily at her and then at the gun he had rested on the ground and was now twirling round.

"Are not you willing to come home with me?"

His voice was smothered, but the gaze he fixed on her became suddenly full and steady.

"Yes, of course I am!" she hastened to reply.

Her eyes rested calmly in his, a flush mantled his cheeks, he shifted his gun to the left hand, extending the right to her.

"Thank you!" whispered he, and gave her hand a warm pressure.

They walked on.

The sole thought she gathered from this, she expatiated on in her own mind, and finally could no longer keep it to herself.

"You do not know my parents."

He walked on some moments before he replied, —

"No; but after you have come home with me, I will have time to become acquainted with them."

"They are so good," she added.

"So I have heard from every one."

He said this firmly but coldly.

Before she had time to think or speak again

he began to tell her about *his* home, about his brothers and sisters, about the poverty they had all worked their way up from, about how capable, true, and cheerful his brothers and sisters were, about the summer visitors and the employment they furnished, about the buildings on the place, and especially the new house he would now erect, and which should be for themselves, and how she should have the supervision of everything, but also plenty of help; indeed, every one would be perfectly devoted to her, and he not least of all! While he was talking they quickened their pace; he spoke with warmth, came closer to her, and when he got through they were walking hand in hand.

Yes, truly; his love for his home and his people made an impression on her, and the unknown attracted, but there was something, nevertheless, something that seemed like a wrong to her own tender-hearted parents. She began therefore anew, —

"But, Hans! Mother is growing old and father is still older; they have suffered much — they need help; they have toiled hard, and" — She either would not or could not say more

He slackened his speed and looked smiling at her.

"Mildred, you mean to say that the gard is intended for you?"

She flushed, but made no reply.

"Ah, well — sufficient unto the day is the evil thereof! But if they ever want to have us take their places, it is *they* who must request it of *us*."

He said this tenderly; but she knew very well all that it signified! Cautious as she was, and accustomed to consider the thoughts of others before her own, she submitted. But it was not long now before they got so far on their way that they could see Tingvold lying at their feet. And then her eyes wandered from the gard up to him, as though it should speak for itself! The broad, bright hill-slopes, encircled by the forest, the buildings, spread out so peacefully in the subdued sunshine, but so large and substantial, looked very beautiful. The valley lay below, the noisy stream meandered through it, gard after gard might be seen down on the plain, and on the opposite side of the valley and gard after gard on *this* side, but none of them, not a single one, equal to Tingvold, none so fruitful, none so imposing to the eye, not one so sheltered in its own home-like comfort, and yet so sparkling on every side! When she saw that he was affected by the sight, she colored with pleasure.

"Yes," answered he, for she had actually asked a question! "Yes, it is true, Tingvold is a fine gard; it has scarcely its match." He smiled and bowed over her. "But I care more for you, Mildred, than for Tingvold; may I not hope that you, too, care more for me than for Tingvold?"

Since this was the way he took it, there was nothing left to her but silence. Moreover, he looked so happy, and he sat down, and she seated herself at his side.

"Now I will sing something for you," he whispered.

She felt happy.

"I have never heard you sing," said she.

"No, you have not; and although my singing is talked about a good deal, you must not expect anything remarkable, for all that there is about it is that I feel myself, *now*, I *must* sing."

And after sitting and meditating a while, he sang his bridal song to the tune of the family march. He sang very softly, but such an exultant tone she had never heard in any voice! The gard lay before her, the gard from which the procession would start; she followed the road with her eyes all the way to the bridge across the stream, then followed the road on the other side as far as the church, into the

birch forest up on a hill, and the cluster of
gards near at hand. The view was not a brilliant one, for the day was not clear; but thus it
best suited the subdued vision of her dreams:
for how many hundred times had she not taken
this churchward journey in her thoughts, only
she had not known with whom! The words
and the tune enchanted her; the peculiar,
warm, quiet voice stirred the depths of her nature; her eyes were full, but she did not weep,
neither did she laugh; but with her hand in
his she sat and looked, now at him, now at the
landscape before her; and when while thus engaged the smoke curled up from the chimney
at home at the first kindling of the fire that
was to boil the noonday pot, she turned and
pointed. Hans had just finished his song and
now he also sat quietly gazing at the prospect.

A little while later, they were once more
journeying onward through the birch forest,
and Hans had some difficulty in keeping his
dog still. Mildred's heart began to throb.
Hans agreed with her that he would wait near
by, and that she should go forward alone. He
carried her over a few swampy places, and he
felt that her hand was moist.

"Do not think about what you are going to
say," he whispered; "just let the words come
as they will of themselves."

She did not utter a word in reply, neither did she look at him. They emerged from the forest, which here consisted of tall, solemn firs, among which they had been slowly walking while he told her in a whisper about her great-grandfather's wooing of his father's sister Aslaug, marvelous stories which she only half heard, but which nevertheless gave her strength, — they emerged from the forest into the dawning light of the meadows and grain fields, and then even he became silent. Now she raised her eyes to his face, and her fear was so apparent and so great, that he became very anxious. He could find no words to bring to her aid, — the case was too fully his own. They walked side by side; some brushwood just opposite the house concealed them from the occupants. When they got so far that he thought she ought to go on alone, he whistled softly to his dog, and Mildred understood this to be a sign that they must part. She paused, looking so unhappy and desolate that he had to whisper, —

"I will pray for you here, Mildred; and then I will come when you need me."

Her eyes expressed her thanks, but not wholly, for she could neither think nor see clearly. And thus she went home. As soon as she had advanced beyond the bushes, she could see right into the large sitting-room in the main building, indeed, clean through it, for the room had windows on either side, overlooking both the forest above and the parish below. Hans, meanwhile, seated himself behind the nearest clump of bushes, with the dog at his side, and so he could see everything in the sitting-room as well as she; but the room was now unoccupied. She looked round once when she came to the barn; then he nodded to her. She turned the corner of the barn, and entered the farm-yard.

Here all was in the old accustomed order, and stillness reigned. Some hens were walking about on the barn-bridge. Up toward the store-house wall to the left the poles, used for drying hay and grain, had been brought forward since she went away; — she saw no other change. She longed to turn to the right to her grandmother's house; it was no doubt her fright that made her desire this respite before the interview with her parents; but there by the chopping-block between the two houses stood her father shafting an axe. He wore a knit jacket, with his suspenders outside. His head was bare; his long thin hair was blown over his face by the breeze that was just begin ning to sweep u from the valley. He looked so well, almost cheerful over his work, that the sight of him inspired her with courage. He did not notice her, so quietly and cautiously had she come walking up over the chips.

"Good day!" she whispered.

He looked at her for a moment, in surprise.

"Dear me! Is that you? Is anything amiss?" he added hurriedly, and gazed searchingly into her face.

"No," said she, coloring slightly.

But his eyes remained fastened on hers, which she did not dare raise. He put aside his axe.

"Let us go in to mother," said he.

On the way to the house, he asked various questions in regard to the work at the sæter, and obtained satisfactory replies. "Now Hans sees us go in," thought Mildred, as they advanced through the opening between the barn and the store-house, on the other side. When they entered the house, her father went to the kitchen door and opened it.

"You will have to come in, mother," said he, through the door; "Mildred is here."

"Dear me! Is anything the matter?" was answered from the kitchen.

"No," replied Mildred, from behind her father, coming forward to the door herself, and then going out to her mother, who sat in front of the hearth, peeling potatoes and putting them into the pot.

Mildred's mother now scrutinized her face as closely as her father had done, and with the same effect. Randi rose, and after setting aside the dish she held, she went to the opposide door, gave some orders outside, retraced her steps, took off her kitchen apron, washed her hands and came forward. They all repaired to the sitting-room.

Mildred knew her parents well, so she was sure that these preparations betokened that they themselves expected something more than common. Her courage had not been great before, and now it grew less. Her father sat down in the high seat, close by the farthest window, which faced the parish. Her mother had seated herself on the same bench, but nearer to the kitchen door. Mildred took her place on the first seat, that is to say, on the long bench in front of the table. Hans could see her there; he could also look right into her father's face, but he did not have so good a view of her mother.

Her mother asked, as the father had done before, about the sæter, obtained the same in formation and a little more, for she inquired more into particulars. Although it was evident that both parties were spinning out the conversation, the theme was soon exhausted. In the silence that ensued both parents looked at Mildred. She avoided their eyes, and inquired about the news of the parish. Although this theme was dragged out to the utmost, *it*, also, came to an end. Then the same silence, the same expectant look in the eyes of the parents. Mildred had no more questions to ask, but began stroking with the palm of her hand the bench on which she was sitting.

"Have you been to your grandmother's?" inquired the mother; she was beginning to be alarmed.

No, Mildred had not. This was an acknowledgment that she had come *here* on a definite errand, and she felt that it could be delayed no longer with propriety.

"There is something that it is my duty to tell you," the young girl faltered at last, her color coming and going and her eyes cast down. Her parents exchanged troubled glances. Mildred raised her head and fixed on them a pair of wide-open, beseeching eyes.

"What is it, my child?" her mother anxiously asked, as she met her gaze.

"I am betrothed," said Mildred, bowing her head and bursting into tears.

A more stunning blow could not have fallen on the little circle! Pale, silent, the parents looked at each other. Their steady, gentle Mildred, for whose prudence and obedience they had so often thanked God, had, without their advice, without their knowledge, taken life's most important step, one which also determined the parents' past and future. Mildred, meanwhile, felt every thought that was working in their minds, and fear checked her tears. Gently, slowly, her father asked, —

"To whom, my child?"

After a pause the answer came in a whisper, —

"It is to Hans Haugen."

The name Haugen had not been mentioned in this house for more than twenty years, nor any circumstance connected therewith. From the stand-point the parents took, only harm had come from Haugen to this gard. Mildred again divined their thoughts; she sat motionless, awaiting her doom. But mildly and slowly once more the father said, —

"We do not know this man; neither your mother nor I. Nor were we aware that you knew him."

"No, neither did I know him," said Mildred.

The astonished parents looked at each other.

"How did this happen, then?"

It was the mother who spoke.

"Oh, I do not know myself," said Mildred.

"Why, dear child, we ought to be able to control our actions."

Mildred made no reply.

"We thought," added the father, meekly, "that we could trust *you*."

Mildred still made no reply.

"But how did it happen?" repeated the mother, more zealously. "You must surely know."

"No, I do not know. I only know that I could not help it; no, indeed, I could not. She sat clinging with both hands to the bench as she spoke.

"God have mercy on you, then! What can have come over you?"

Mildred made no reply. Once more the father had a subduing influence on the conversation. In a calm, friendly tone, he asked, —

"Why did you not speak to one of us, my child?"

The mother, too, fell into this vein, and said quietly, —

"You know how fond we are of our children, we, who have lived so lonely a life; and we may well say, of you, in especial, Mildred, for you have been dearer than all else to us."

Mildred scarcely knew where she was sitting.

"No, we did not think that you would forsake us thus."

It was the father who spoke. Hushed though his voice was, it pained none the less.

"I will not forsake you," she faltered.

"You must not say so," he answered, more gravely than he had yet spoken," for you have already left us."

Mildred felt that this was true, and yet it was *not* true; but she could not explain this. Her mother said, —

"Of what avail is it to us that we have led a loving, pious life with our children? At the first temptation "— For her daughter's sake she refrained from saying more.

But Mildred could not stand this any longer.

"I will not forsake you," she cried. "I do not want to grieve you. I only could not — no I could not!" and flinging herself down on the table with her face toward her father, and her head on her arm, she sobbed aloud.

Neither of her parents had the heart to in

crease with a single reproach the sorrow she evidently felt. Consequently a hush fell upon the room. It might have lasted a long time; but Hans Haugen noticed from his hiding-place that Mildred needed help. His huntsman's eye had seen her cast herself down on the table, and he sprang to his feet; soon his light step was heard in the passage. He knocked; every eye was fixed on the door; but no one said: "Come in!" Mildred half rose, her face red with weeping; the door opened, Hans, with his gun and dog, stood on the threshold, pale but calm, turned and closed the door, while the dog walked, wagging its tail, to Mildred. Hans' thoughts had been too much occupied to observe that the dog followed him.

"Good-day!" said he. Mildred sank back in her seat, drew a long breath, and looked at him, relieved; her fright, her bad conscience, was all gone, she *was right, yes, indeed, she was right*, — now God's will be done!

No one had responded to his greeting; nor had any one asked him to come forward.

"I am Hans Haugen," said he, calmly; and he rested his gun on the floor, and stood holding it. After the parents had exchanged glances a few times, he continued, but with an effort: "I came here with Mildred; for if she has done wrong, the fault is mine."

Something must be said; the mother looked at the father, and he said, finally, that this had come about without their knowledge, nor could Mildred give any explanation of how it had happened. But Hans replied that he could give none either.

"I am no boy," said he, "for I am twenty-eight years old, and yet this came about in such a way that I, who never thought of any one before, could not think of anything else in the world from the moment I saw her. Had she said no — ah, I do not know — but I certainly never would have amounted to very much afterward."

The calm, truthful way in which he said this, was good to hear; Mildred trembled in her seat, for she knew that his words presented a new view of the case. He had his cap on, for it was not customary in this valley for a stranger to take off his cap on entering a house; but now he involuntarily removed it, hung it on the barrel of his gun and held his hands over it. There was something in the young man's whole manner that demanded courtesy.

"Young as Mildred is," said the mother, "none of us thought that she would so soon begin to enter into anything of this sort."

"That may be true; but then you know I

am much older," replied he, "and the management of affairs at my house is not very extensive; it will not require great effort, and I have plenty of help."

The parents looked at each other, at Mildred, at him.

"Would she have to go home with you?" asked the father incredulously, almost scornfully.

"Yes," said Hans; "it is not the gard I am courting."

He flushed; Mildred did the same.

If the gard had sunk into the earth, it could not have astonished the parents more than to have it disdained, and Mildred's silence showed them that she agreed with Hans. At all events, this decision of the young people was something wholly beyond the calculations of the parents; they felt themselves humiliated.

"It was you who said you would not forsake us," remarked the mother in quiet reproach, and her words struck home.

But Hans came to Mildred's aid.

"Forsake you? Why, every child who marries must leave its parents." He smiled, and added, in a kindly tone, "The distance is not great; it is but little over five miles from here to Haugen."

Words, however, are of but little avail on such occasions; thoughts will take their course in spite of them. Mildred's parents felt forsaken, aye, betrayed, by the determination of the young people. That it was possible to live comfortably at Haugen they knew very well; travelers who visited the place had given it a name; there had even now and then been something about it in the papers; but still Haugen was Haugen, and that *Mildred*, their favorite child, should take the family's journey back to Haugen, it was too much! Under such circumstances others would perhaps have been angry, but these two preferred to avoid what they did not like. They exchanged significant looks, and the father said, mildly, —

"This is too much at once, we are unable to answer yet."

"No," joined in the mother; "we had not expected such important news; nor to receive it in this way."

Hans hesitated a little before he said, —

"It is true that Mildred should have asked her parents first. But how, if neither of us knew of it before it was too late? That is really the way it was. So we could not do any thing else than come, both of us, as soon as we were engaged, and that we have done. You must not be too severe."

After this there was nothing to be said on the score of their conduct, and his calm way of speaking gave force to his words. On the whole, the father noticed that he was not an equal match to Hans, and so small was the confidence he had in himself he felt anxious to drop the question.

"We do not know you," said he, and looked at his wife; "we must have time to consider."

"Yes, that is certainly best," observed Randi, "for we ought to know the person to whom we give our daughter."

Mildred felt the indignity of this remark, but she looked imploringly at Hans.

"That is true," replied Hans, and began with one hand to twirl his gun, "although I do not think there are many in the parish who are very much better known than I. But perhaps some one has been speaking ill of me?"

He looked up at them. Mildred felt embarrassed for her parents, and they felt that they had possibly awakened suspicion, and this they did not wish.

"No, we have heard nothing against you," both exclaimed in a breath, and the mother hastened to add, that the fact was they did not know him because they had so seldom heard anything about the Haugen family.

She meant no harm in the least by this; but no sooner had the words crossed her lips than she realized that they were not happily expressed, and she noticed that both her husband and Mildred thought the same. There was some delay before the answer came.

"If the house of Tingvold has failed to inquire after the Haugen family, the fault is not ours; for we have been poor people until lately."

There was a reproach in these words that all three felt to be true, and that profoundly so. But never until now had it occurred to the husband and wife, reserved and absorbed in their sorrow as they had been, that they had neglected a duty; never until now had they considered that their poor relatives at Haugen should not have been made to suffer for misfortunes for which they were in nowise to blame. They stole shy glances at each other, and kept their seats, covered with shame. Hans had spoken cautiously, although the mother's answer could not but have annoyed him. Both parents felt then that they had a noble man before them, and that in a double sense they had something to make amends for. And so the father said, —

"Let us take a little more time. Cannot

you stay to dinner with us? Then we can have a chance to talk a little."

" You must come and sit down," added the mother.

Both rose.

Hans put aside his gun, with his cap on it, and crossed the floor to where Mildred sat; she at once rose, she knew not herself why. The mother said there was a good deal to be seen to in the kitchen, and left the room. The father acted as if he were about to follow her example; but Mildred, not wishing to be alone with Hans as long as her parents refused their consent, quickly moved to the other door. They saw her walking across the farm-yard toward her grandmother's dwelling. Then the father could not leave Hans alone, so he turned and sat down.

The two men talked together about indifferent matters; first of all about the hunting, and about their affairs on the mountain in the summer huts; about the income from such sources, and much more to like effect. Afterwards they came to Haugen and the tourists that found their way there, to the cultivation of the soil in these upland regions; and all that the father heard gave him the impression that everything was going on well and pros perously at Haugen. The mother, coming and going with her preparations for dinner, often had occasion to listen, and it was very evident that the shyness of the old people was gradually becoming transformed into confidence; for the questions began to grow more to the point.

They all noticed Hans's good manners at table. He sat at the wall, just opposite Mildred and her mother; while the father sat at the end of the table in the high seat. The farm people had had their dinner earlier, and in the kitchen where the family themselves usually ate with them. But the fact probably was that on this occasion they did not care to have Hans seen. At table Mildred felt that her mother looked at her whenever Hans smiled. He was one of those grave-looking people whose faces light up pleasantly when they smile. Several such things she put together to form the result her heart was set on having. But she felt so uncertain about matters that the atmosphere of suspense in the room was so oppresive to her, that she for her part longed to get away, and after dinner she went again to her grandmother's.

The men took a turn round the gard, but so directing their steps that they did not come either where the farm laborers were, or where the grandmother could see them. Later they sat down in the sitting-room again, and by this time the mother was through with her work and could join them. The conversation became by degrees more confidential, as might have been expected, and as time wore on (yet, to be sure, not before evening) the mother ventured to beg Hans to tell how it had all come about between him and Mildred, as Mildred had herself been unable to give any information. Perhaps it was chiefly feminine curiosity that led the mother to ask this, but to Hans the question was exceedingly welcome.

He gave no account of the first interview, for he could not do so; but in full details and with profound joy he narrated the events of the previous day, telling of Beret's stormy march in search of him, because Mildred was distracted with anguish of mind on her parents' account; and when he came to Mildred herself and depicted her flight toward home, and how, exhausted in soul and body, she had been compelled to rest, and had fallen asleep, desolate and unhappy, — then it seemed to the old people that they recognized their child once more. They could not avoid feeling, especially the mother, that they had been too severe.

But while the young mar talked about Mil

dred, he was telling, without being aware of it, about himself; for his love for Mildred glowed from every word and made the parents glad. He grew conscious of this at last and became happy himself; and these two, who were unaccustomed to such unbroken heartiness and strength, felt genuine happiness. This kept continually increasing, until the mother involuntarily exclaimed, smiling, —

"Why, I really believe you got as far as the wedding, you two, before either of us were consulted."

The father chimed in with a laugh in order to help the question, and Hans replied, as seemed appropriate to the occasion, by softly humming a single line of the bridal march, —

"Speed us on, speed us on, we're in haste, you and I," —

and laughed, but was discreet enough to turn the conversation at once to something else. By a mere chance he looked up at Randi and saw that she was very pale. In a moment he felt that he had done something wrong in reminding her of this tune, and that just now. Endrid looked anxiously at his wife, whose agitation kept increasing until it had risen to such a pitch that she could no longer remain in the room; she rose and went out.

"I am afraid I have done wrong," said Hans, in alarm.

Endrid made no reply. Thoroughly distressed, Hans rose to follow Mildred's mother and offer her an apology, but sat down again, protesting that he had not meant the least harm.

"Oh, you could not be expected to know," answered Endrid.

"Cannot you go after her and make all right again?"

He had acquired such confidence in this man that he felt at perfect liberty to ask this of him. But Endrid replied, —

"No; let her alone; I know her."

Hans, who had a little while before felt almost at the goal of his wishes, was now plunged in disappointment, and could not be coaxed into good spirits again, although the father exercised the utmost patience in trying to cheer him. The dog lent his aid, by coming forward and joining them, for Endrid had asked repeatedly about it and afterwards given a detailed account of a dog *he* had once owned, and whose ways he had closely observed, as solitary people are wont to do.

Now Randi had gone outside of the door, and seated herself on the flag-stone. Her daugh ter's betrothed had caused the bridal march to jar more than ever the memories she bore within her. *She* had not, like her daughter, given herself to a man whom she loved! The shame of her ride to church had been just, for she had not been sitting in perfect truth at her bridegroom's side. The mortification and grief, the loss of her children, the long years of suffering and conflict, all rushed over her. All she had read and prayed over this pain had then been of no avail, for the most violent agitation now overpowered her! That this could happen to her, cast her despairingly down into the depths of self-accusation; she felt the scorn of the people over her false churchward ride; she again scourged her own impotence, that she could not stop her tears that time, her memories now; that through her lack of self-control she had put her parents in a false light, destroyed her own health, and thereby murdered the children she bore,—all the time feigning a piety she did not feel, for she was sure of this now. Oh, to think she had progressed no farther than this! So wretched, so pitiably wretched she felt, that she did not dare look up to God; for how had she not disappointed herself and Him! But wherefore, she was forced to ask, wherefore call to light just now al the hatefulness that had coiled itself about her inner being? Was she envious of Mildred? Envious of her own daughter? No, she was not, she knew she was not, and she began to hold up her head once more! Now her sin should be atoned for by her daughter. What a glorious thought! Could our children atone for our sins? Yes, as truly as they are a work of our own, they could, for the truth that was in Mildred, the mother, frail as she was, had fostered. But in order to profit thereby she must enter into it herself in repentance, in gratitude! And before Randi knew how it was herself, she could pray again, could bend in profound humility and contrition before the Lord, who had once more revealed to her what she was without Him. She prayed for mercy, as those pray who are petitioning for their lives, for now she would have life again; this she felt! Now her debt was cancelled; this had been the final settlement, she was merely overwhelmed by it! And she rose and looked up, while the tears streamed down her cheeks: she felt at ease; there was One who had lifted her burden from her! But had she not often felt thus before? No, never as she did now, her first victory had just been won! And she advanced farther and she felt this: she belonged to herself! Something was rent asunder that until now had held her in bondage; through every motion she made she felt that now she was free, soul and body! If, next to God, she must thank her daughter for this, why, then, to Mildred must be granted the full enjoyment of her happiness! She came to the porch of grandmother's house; but none of those within recognized her step. She took hold of the latch and opened the door, as though she were another person.

"Mildred, come here!" said she, and Mildred and the grandmother looked at each other, for this surely was not Mildred's mother.

Mildred sprang forward. What could be the matter? Her mother drew her forward by the arm, closed the door behind her so that they were alone, and then flung herself on her daughter's neck and wept and wept, while she embraced her with vigor and an intensity of bliss, which Mildred, exalted by her love, could return with all her heart.

"God forever bless and reward you!" whispered her mother.

The two in the family sitting-room saw them coming walking across the yard, hand in hand, and they saw, moreover, that their coming was prophetic. The door was opened, they both entered and came forward. But instead of giving Mildred to Hans, or saying anything to the father or to him, Randi merely clasped her daughter in her arms again, and in a fresh burst of emotion, once more cried, —

"God forever bless and reward you!"

A little while later all four sat in the grandmother's room. The old lady was very happy; she had for a long time past been kept posted by the young people in regard to Hans Haugen, and she comprehended at once that this alliance would serve as an atonement in the lives of her son and daughter-in-law. Moreover, the light-hearted old lady thought Hans was extremely handsome! They all remained with her, and the day ended by the father, after singing a psalm, reading from a prayer-book a passage beginning: "The Lord has been in our house."

Of the remainder of their lives I shall only single out two days, and of these but a few moments in each.

The first is the wedding-day of the young people. Inga, Mildred's cousin, who was now herself a wife, had come to attend to the adornment of the bride. This was done in the storehouse; the old chest, in which the bridal silver was kept, — the crown, the belt, the buckle, the brooches, the rings, — was brought forward. Grandmother had the key to it, she was there herself to open it, and Beret was with her, as her assistant. Mildred had already decked herself in her bridal dress, and all the finery that belonged to her, when this splendor (which Beret and the grandmother had polished the week before) was brought to light, glittering and heavy. Article after article was tried on. Beret held the glass for the bride. The old lady told how so many of her family had worn this silver on their wedding-day, and how the happiest of all had been her own mother, Aslaug Haugen.

Just then the old family bridal march was heard outside: every one in the store-house paused, listened, then hastened to the door to see what was going on. The first person their eyes fell on was Endrid, the bride's father. He had seen Hans Haugen, and his brothers and sisters, come riding toward the gard; it was a rare thing for Endrid to have any unusual ideas; but this time it occurred to him that these guests should be received with the ancestral tune. He gave the fiddlers orders to go forward playing it; and there he now stood himself in their midst near the store-house, holding in his hand a silver tankard filled with the wedding ale. Several others had joined him. Hans and his faithful brothers and sisters drove into the gard and it was very evident that this reception touched them.

An hour later, as a matter of course, the bridal march was struck up again; that was when the bride and bridegroom, and the bride's parents, and grandmother and Beret, and the bridegroom's brothers and sisters came out in couples, with the fiddlers at their head, to get into the carts. There are moments in our lives when all signs are favorable, and at such a moment the bridal party drove forth from Tingvold one bright spring day. At church there was assembled so great a multitude of people that no one remembered ever having seen anything to equal it. Every one in the crowd knew the family history, and how it was interwoven with this bridal march which now rang out jubilantly through the glad sunshine, its tones encircling the bride and bridegroom, and the happy bridal party.

And because all their thoughts centred in this one, the priest, too, chose a text for the wedding discourse that afforded him an opportunity of dwelling on the idea that children are the crowning glory of our lives when they are a reflection of *our* honor, our development, our labor.

On the way out of the church Hans paused in front of the church door; he said something; the bride, in her supreme happiness, did not hear what it was, but she divined its meaning. He wanted her to look at Ole Haugen's grave, which was richly decked with flowers. She did so, and they passed out of the churchyard in such a way that their garments touched the head-board of his grave. The parents followed.

The other moment of their lives which must here be unveiled, relates to the first visit of Endrid and Randi as grandparents. Hans had had his way, and the newly-married couple were established at Haugen, although he had been obliged to promise that he would take Tingvold when the old people either could not or did not wish to manage it longer, and when the ancient grandmother was dead. During this whole visit, however, there is but one occurrence that concerns the readers of this story; this is, that when Randi, after having been affectionately received and after partaking of the refreshments that were brought forward, sat with her daughter's little child in her lap, she began to rock it in her arms and hum something over it and that was the bridal march. Her daughter clasped her hands in surprise, but controlled herself immediately, and said nothing. Hans invited Endrid to let him fill his glass again, which Endrid declined, but this was only an excuse on both sides to exchange glances.

CAPTAIN MANSANA.

INTRODUCTION TO CAPTAIN MANSANA.

The following story appeared some years ago in a Danish Christmas Gift, "Fra Fjæld og Dal" (From Mountain and Valley), collected by Hr. H. J. Greensteen. In German the work has already passed through two editions, and many have requested that it might be published in a separate volume in our language also.

Certain comments in the criticism of the public press of Denmark and Sweden lead me to make the following explanations: The narrative is in all essentials historic; above all, the most novel of its incidents are historic — some of them even to their most minute details. Captain Mansana is drawn from life; what he is said to have performed, he really did perform, and the singular destiny ascribed to him is historically his in all that has a determining influence on his psychological development.

What induced me to make this presentation of his character may be found in a few lines of Theresa's letter, which concludes this story.

Compare her testimony concerning Mansana with the delineation of the character of Lassalle, published at the same time by Dr. Georg Brandes in his "The Nineteenth Century," and you will observe that the most secret impelling forces of Lassalle's destiny — which Brandes has depicted with so masterly a hand — are the same as those which controlled Mansana. Lassalle's rich intellectual powers, strong individuality, and great activity are naturally of far higher interest; but the character-phenomenon is the same, and it entertained me, in its day, that we should both have had our attention drawn to this at the same time.

BJÖRNSTJERNE BJÖRNSON.

CAPTAIN MANSANA

CHAPTER I.

As I was stepping into a railway car at Bologna, on a journey to Rome, I bought some daily papers. Among these was a newspaper from Florence, containing a letter from Rome, that soon engrossed my undivided attention, for it carried me back thirteen years to an earlier visit to Rome and to my hosts in a little town in the vicinity of the capital, which at that time belonged to the Pope. The letter announced that the bones of the patriot Mansana, who had been buried in the malefactors' graveyard at Rome, had now, in response to a petition from his native town, been disinterred, and would, in the course of a few days, be received by the authorities of that town, and attended by delegates from various societies of Rome and the adjacent towns to A——, Mansana's birthplace. A monument and solemn festal reception awaited them there; the martyr was to have accorded him a tardy recompense.

Now I had lodged in this Mansana's house thirteen years previous to this; his wife and his younger brother's wife were my hostesses; of the brothers themselves, the elder was a captive in Rome, the younger an exile in Genoa.

The letter, furthermore, depicted the career of the elder Mansana. With the exception of the last portion, I knew it before, and that was just what increased my desire to join the procession which on the following Sunday was to start from the Piazza Barberini in Rome and end at A——.

And so on Sunday morning, at seven o'clock, one gray October day, I found myself at the appointed place. There were gathered together a multiplicity of banners, accompanied by those men, as a rule six, which each society had selected for the purpose. My eyes were fixed on a banner bearing the inscription, "The Struggle for the Fatherland," and to the accompanying forms, in red shirts, with sashes about their waists, cloaks thrown over their shoulders, pantaloons thrust into their boot-tops, and broad hats, with floating plumes. What countenances! What wills! Those who have seen the usual portrait of Orsini — he who threw bombs at Napoleon the Third — well know the Italian type of countenance belonging to the men who rose in their might against the tyranny of state and church, defying prisons and places of execution, banding together in formidable associations, progenitors of the army that freed Italy. Napoleon had been a member of such a society. He, as well as the rest of his comrades, had sworn that he would use whatever position he might attain for Italy's unity and welfare, or, in the opposite case, would forfeit his life. Now when Napoleon became Emperor of France, it was the Carbonari comrade Orsini who reminded him of his oath. It was done in such a way, too, that Napoleon knew what he had to expect if he failed to keep it.

The impression Orsini's portrait made on me the first time I saw it was that ten thousand such men might conquer the world. And here I was in the presence of some of these men who were endowed by the same public need with the same will. There had fallen a certain repose over the wills now; but something dark about the eyes told that it was not that of peace. The medals on their breasts showed that they had been present at Porte San Pancrazio in 1849 when Garibaldi twice repulsed superior numbers of Frenchmen; in 1858, at Lake Guarda

and in 1859, in Sicily and at Naples. And what
the medals did not relate, also belonged, in all
likelihood, to the history of their lives, namely,
that they had fought at Mentana. It is just
such battle-fields as the latter, unrecognized by
the government, that are most deeply branded
into the souls of the people. Napoleon was
made to feel this after he had secured the aid
of Italy against Germany; it was Mentana that
forbade the king and the government to redeem
their pledge : to have done so would have cost
a crown.

The contrast between the dark, appalling
will of the Italian people and their mocking
levity or absolute indifference, is quite as great
as the contrast between these men of Orsini-
like will whom I here saw and the frivolous
countenances, expressing either refined scorn
or total apathy, among the surrounding spectators, as well as among the representatives who
accompanied the banners, bearing such inscrip-
tions as " The Press," " Free Thought," " Free
Labor," etc., etc. Involuntarily I thought : it
is the levity of one half that forces the will of
the other half. So great, so universal, had
been this levity, that great in proportion, dark
in proportion must be the will when roused.
And there ran through my mind the history of

Italy in her reckless frivolity and in the decrees of her will. I passed back and forth from Brutus to Orsini, from Catilina to Cesare Borgia, from Lucullus to Leo the Tenth, from Savonarola to Garibaldi, while the multitude was set in motion, banners floated, heralds proclaimed aloud the history of Mansana from the pages and small pamphlets they held in their hands, and the cortège turned into Via Felice. Silence reigned: the lofty houses had but few spectators thus early in the morning, still fewer when the procession wound its way into Via Venti-Settembre, past the Quirinal; but the numbers increased as it descended to the Foro Romano and moved past the Coliseum to the Porta Giovanni. Outside of this the hearse waited. It had been provided by the municipal authorities; servants of the law drove it. Without delay it set forth. Behind the hearse walked two young men, one in civilian's dress, the other wearing the uniform of a Bersaglieri officer. Both were tall, spare, muscular, with small heads and low brows; both alike in form and in face, and yet so infinitely different. They were the sons of the deceased.

I remembered them as boys of thirteen or fourteen, and the circumstance to which my recollections of them clung was curious enough

I remembered their father's aged mother throwing stones after them, and the boys standing at a distance laughing derisively at her. Suddenly I recalled with the utmost distinctness her strong, wrathful eye, her sinewy, but wrinkled hands. I could see her gray hair, bristling about the coffee-colored face; and now as I looked at these boys I could almost have said that the stones she threw had not missed their mark and had become a part of them.

How their grandmother hated them! Had they given her special cause for this? That they had; for hate begets hate, and war war. But at the outset? Yes; I was not with them at the time; but it is not difficult to divine.

She had been early left a widow, this old woman, and in her strong, young beauty she turned the good graces and sympathy of the people into a source of income for herself and her two sons, one of whom now lay in the coffin; the only beings she loved, and that with so "furious" a love that it wearied her sons. When they saw the wiles she employed in availing herself of her privileges as a pretty widow, to obtain benefits for her boys, they despised these benefits also. Once turned from her, they cast their affections on ideal things, such as Italy's freedom, Italy's unity, just as they had been taught by ardent young comrades: their mother's "frenzied" limitations in regard to what was her own, made them daily more enthusiastic to sacrifice everything for the common good. They were not merely as strong as she: they were stronger.

There arose sharp struggles in which she succumbed; yet not entirely before their connections with secret societies had procured for them associations which extended far beyond their native town and the social circle to which her family belonged. Moreover, they each brought home a bride from a more distinguished house than their mother's, with an outfit larger than hers had been, and with a dower which she could not but call handsome. Then she was silenced for a time; it seemed to her that, after all, this being a patriot was not without its advantages.

But the time came when both sons had to flee; when the elder one was captured and cast into prison; when the most monstrous public extortions began; when unjust officials singled out defenseless widows as their prey. The time came when their house had to be mortgaged; then their first vineyard; finally their second. Aye, the time came when the first vineyard was seized by the mortgage holder

And the time came when the two aristocratic wives, who had been friends from childhood, went out to service in the field, in the vineyard, and in houses; when they had to take lodgers and wait upon them; and for all this they were rewarded with words of derision, — not only by the clerical party, who under the papal dominion were the absolute rulers of the city, but by others; for *they* were in the minority who honored wives for the sacrifices their husbands had made, and who united with them in hoping for freedom, enlightenment, and justice. Now the old woman had won! But how? So that she wept over her rejected love, her despised counsel, her lost property; and rising up she cursed the sons who had forsaken and ruined her, until a single glance — no word was ever spoken — from the eldest daughter-in-law drove her back again to the hearth where she was in the habit of sitting, and where she passed her time in idleness when such spells came over her. Before very long she would leave the house, and if she met her grandsons, beneath whose low brows she unluckily thought she saw the bright gleam she had first adored, then feared in her own sons, she would draw them passionately to her, warn them against the ways of their fathers, grossly abuse the rabble, who were unworthy of the sacrifice of a penny, to say nothing of that of welfare, family, freedom; and then she would curse her sons, the boys' fathers; they were the noblest, but at the same time the most ungrateful and most foolish sons that ever mother in that town had given birth to! And the unhappy woman would shake the boys from her, crying, —

"Do be more reasonable, you worthless scamps! Why, you are standing there laughing! Be not like your stupid mothers in there, for they doted on the folly of my boys, — verily, I am surrounded by lunatics!"

And she would push her grandsons away and weep, draw herself up, and then retreat. In after years neither she nor the boys used much ceremony in their dealings with one another. *They* laughed at her when she had one of her attacks, and *she* flung stones at them; and at last matters came to such a pass that if she merely chanced to be sitting alone, the boys would say, "Grandmother, have you gone mad again?" and then the stones would fly.

But why did not the old woman dare speak in the presence of her daughter-in-law? For the same reason that she yielded in the presence of her sons in days of yore. Her husband had been a sickly man, in no condition to manage his property; he had chosen her as the complement of himself. To be sure, she raised the property but she lowered him. *He* had a refined smile, varied culture, and lofty aspirations, and he suffered in her society. His nobler nature she could not destroy, — only his peace of mind and his health. And so it happened that the beauty of character she had despised while he lived, gained the ascendency over her after his death. And when it reappeared as an inspiration in her sons, and as a reproachful reminder in the pure eyes of her daughter-in-law, she was conquered completely.

I say the grandmother's stones had not missed their mark, and were lodged in her grandsons. Look at those two men marching there! The youngest, the one in civilian's dress, had a smile about his rather thin lips, a smile, too, in his small eyes; but I do not believe it would have been well to irritate him. He had been helped on in the world by his father's political friends, had early learned to bow and offer thanks, — I think not, however, through gratitude.

But look at the elder! The same small head, the same low brow, yet both broader. No smile about either lips or eyes. I did not even wish to see him smile. Tall and slim like his brother, he was even more bony; and while both men gave the impression of gymnastic strength, and looked as if they were quite able to leap over the hearse, the elder one gave the additional impression of literally desiring to do so ; for the half lounging gait of the brothers, the evident result of unused powers, had become in the elder an impatient elasticity, — he seemed to walk on springs. His thoughts were apparently absent, for his eyes wandered far beyond all surrounding objects; and when later I offered him my card and reminded him of our former acquaintance, I had proof that this was really the case.

I conversed with several persons in the procession who were from the patriot's town. I inquired after grandmother Mansana. There was a general smile, and several at the same time eagerly told me that she had lived until the previous year: she had reached the age of ninety-five. I perceived that she was understood. It was told me with equal zeal that before her death she had experienced the satisfaction of seeing her home fully her own again : the one vineyard had been repurchased, and both were free from debt, as were also the fields. All was done out of gratitude to the patriot martyr, whose glory was now on all lips it had become the pride of the town ; his life, and that of his brother were, in fact, its sole contribution to the work of deliverance.

So she had lived to see all *this!*

And I inquired after the wives of the two martyrs, and learned that the younger one had succumbed under her calamities, especially her grief at the loss of her only daughter. But the wife of the elder Mansana, the mother of the two young men, was living. The faces of the narrators became grave, their voices hushed, the conversation was ere long conducted by one individual, with occasional additional remarks by the others, all with a certain slow solemnity. She had evidently acquired power over them, this pure woman, with her grand soul. I heard how she had put herself in communication with her husband while he was yet in prison, had informed him that Garibaldi had instigated a revolt within the town and an attack from without, and that the people were waiting for Mansana to be free ; he was to be the leader of the work in Rome. And he became free! He owed this to his own rare strength of will and to his wife's wise fidelity. He feigned insanity, that was her counsel; he shrieked until his voice was gone, then until his strength was exhausted ; for in the mean time he had not taken a mouthful either of food or of drink. Almost at death's door, he persevered in this course, until he was transferred to an insane hospital. His wife could visit him there, and from there they fled — not out of the city; no, the great preparations demanded his presence, and she first waited upon him, afterwards shared his hazardous undertaking. Who else in his place, after so long an imprisonment, would not have sought freedom's soil, when it was but two or three miles distant? But one of those for whom he risked life and all that was his, betrayed him; he was again taken captive, and without him a large part of the plan became fruitless: that is to say, it resulted in defeat on the frontiers; in the conviction, imprisonment or death of thousands in the capital and in the provinces. Before the clock struck the hour of freedom, he had been beheaded and buried amongst his dead fellow-prisoners, thieves and murderers, in the great malefactors' burying ground of the capital — from which to-day his bones had been disinterred.

Now the widow, enveloped in a long black veil, stood waiting for him at the head of the multitude in the flag-adorned church-yard of his native town, beside the already completed monument. That same day, after the new burial, it was to be unveiled amid the thunder of cannon, to which a festal illumination on the mountains, later in the evening, was to give response.

Our way led over the yellow gray Campagna up towards the mountains; we advanced from one mountain town to another, and everywhere there extended, as far as the eye could reach, a human throng, with uncovered heads. The peasantry from the neighboring towns had assembled in haste; choruses of music rang through the narrow streets, streamers and flags hung from every window, garlands fell, flowers were strewed about, handkerchiefs waved, and tears glistened. We soon arrived at Mansana's native town, where the reception was still more affecting, and whither no insignificant portion of the large masses from the other towns had followed us. But the crowd was greatest at the church-yard.

I, however, as a stranger, was favored, and had assigned to me a place not far from the widow. Many wept at sight of her, but she kept her quiet gaze fixed unmovedly on the coffin, the flowers, the multitude. *She* did not weep; for the whole of this combined could not restore to her him whom she had lost, nor did it invest him with increased honor in her eyes

She looked upon it all as upon something that had been known to her for years before this day. How beautiful she was! By this remark I do not mean to refer only to the noble lines which could never be wholly obliterated in a face or in eyes which had once been the most beautiful in the town, indeed were still so when I saw her thirteen years before this, although even then she showed traces of having wept too much. No, I refer also to the actual halo of truth that surrounded her form, movements, countenance, gaze. It made itself manifest in the same way as the light, and like this it transfigured whatever it fell upon.

I shall never forget the meeting between her and her sons. They both embraced and kissed her; she held them each in turn long in her arms, as though she were praying over them. A hush fell over all, some involuntarily removed their hats. The younger son, whom she first embraced, drew back, with his handkerchief to his eyes. The elder stood still, for she looked at him — aye, looked at him; *every* eye was turned on him, and he colored deeply. There was unspeakable pain in that look, an unfathomable prophecy. How often I have since recalled it! With his face dyed crimson, he firmly returned her gaze, and she looked away that she might not goad him to defiance. It was quite apparent that this was so. The tendencies of the two families stood face to face.

CHAPTER II.

On the way back, it was not the touching revelation of the mother that was most prominent in all I had experienced, it was the Bersaglieri officer's defiant countenance, his tall, bony form, and athletic bearing. And thus it was that I could not help inquiring about him. To my surprise, I found that it was the daring exploits of this son that had again drawn attention to the father, and called forth the honor so late accorded to his memory. I had fallen upon something genuinely Italian. Concerning father, mother, speeches, reception, beauties of scenery surrounding the last solemnities at the church-yard, torchlights in the mountains, — of all these things not a word was spoken! Until we parted in Rome, we were entertained with anecdotes about the Bersaglieri officer.

When yet a boy he had been with Garibaldi and had won favor to such a degree that later he was kept at a military school by his own and his father's friends.

A command was intrusted to him, as to so many Italians in those days, before the final examination was passed, and soon he had so distinguished himself that he received a permanent appointment. One solitary deed bore his name over Italy, even before he had been in a battle. He was one of a reconnoitring party, and having wound his way by chance and alone up to the top of a wooded height, he espied, in a thicket behind it, a horse, soon another, drew nearer, saw a traveling carriage, came still closer, and discovered a group of people, a lady and two servants encamped in the grass. He promptly recognized them. The lady had the previous day come driving toward the vanguard, seeking refuge from the enemy, of whom she declared herself afraid. She had been allowed to pass; and now she had returned by another route, and she and her servants were seeking repose in this spot. The horses had an ill-used look; they had been driven the whole night, and that so hard that it was impossible to progress without first having some rest. All this Mansana read, as it were, at a glance.

It was on a Sunday morning; the Italian troops were in camp; mass had just been read, and they were at breakfast when the outposts saw young Mansana coming galloping toward them with a lady on the pommel of his saddle and two unharnessed horses fastened to the latter. The lady was a spy from the enemy's army; her "two servants," officers of the hostile force, lay wounded in the woods. The lady was recognized at once, and Mansana's "Evviva!" reëchoed by thousands. The troops broke up; the enemy must be near at hand, and it was soon ascertained that this Giuseppe Mansana's presence of mind had saved the vanguard from falling into a snare.

I shall tell many anecdotes about him; but in order that they may be understood, I must begin by stating that he was the first gymnast and fencer in the army. Both now and later I heard but one opinion of this.

Immediately after the war he was in garrison at Florence. One day it was told at an officers' café that a Belgian officer, who a few weeks before had been stationed there, had proved to be in reality a papal officer, and now amused himself among his comrades in Rome by making sport of the Italian officers, whom, with a few exceptions, he pronounced mere ignorant parade puppets, whose main characteristic was childish vanity. This story excited much in dignation among the officers of the garrison in Florence, and from the café where he had heard it young Mansana went at once to the colonel and asked for a six days' furlough. This was granted him. He went home, purchased civilian's clothes, and without delay took the direct route to Rome. By the way of the forest he crossed the frontier, and on the third day appeared in the officers' café in Rome, near the Piazza Colonna, where he soon saw sitting before him the Belgian papal officer. He walked up to the latter and quietly bade him follow him outside. Here Mansana told the officer who he was, bade him take a friend and accompany him beyond the gates, to give satisfaction to the Italian corps of officers in a duel with him. So frankly and completely did Mansana trust to the honor of this man that the latter could not fail him. He immediately went in after a friend, and three hours later was a corpse. But young Mansana set out forthwith on his return route through the forest to Florence. Not by him was the affair made known in Florence, where, meanwhile, he had remained, but through tidings from Rome, and he was sentenced to a long imprisonment for having left the town without permission and for having furthermore been in another country; but the officers made a banquet for him when he was free and the king honored him with a decoration.

Shortly afterward he was stationed at a Salerno garrison. Smuggling had become rife on the coast, and the troops were aiding in putting a stop to it. In civilian's dress he went out to make observations, and learned at an inn that a ship carrying smuggled goods was now lying out beyond the range of vision, and was to near the coast under the cover of night. He went home, changed his clothes, took with him two chosen men, and toward evening they all three rowed out in a frail little boat. I heard this anecdote told and confirmed on the spot. I have heard it since from others; and later had the opportunity of reading it in the newspapers; but nevertheless it always remains incomprehensible to me, how in boarding a vessel with his two followers he could compel sixteen — sixteen — men to obedience, as he did, and bring the ship to the wharf!

After the capture of Rome, in which he also took part, and where he worked miracles, especially during the inundation which followed, he was sitting one evening in the same officers' café, in front of which he had challenged the Belgian papal officer. He there heard some brother officers who had just come from a social gathering, telling about a Hungarian who had drank too much Italian wine, and under its inspiring influence had fallen to boasting about the Hungarians, to such an extent that, after some slight opposition, he had even gone so far as to assert that three Italians would be welcome to attack one Hungarian! All the officers laughed with those who were telling this, all with the exception of Giuseppe Mansana.

"Where does this Hungarian lodge?" asked he.

His tone was one of utter indifference; he neither looked up nor removed the cigarette from his mouth. The Hungarian had been followed home, so the desired information was at once given. Mansana rose.

"Are you going?" asked they.

"To be sure," he replied.

"But surely not to the Hungarian?" some one inquired, good-naturedly.

Now there was nothing good-natured about Giuseppe Mansana.

"Where else?" cried he, and strode away.

The rest rose at once to accompany him. They endeavored on the way to make him sensible of the fact that a drunken man could not be called to account.

"Do not be alarmed," was Mansana's response, "I shall treat him accordingly."

The Hungarian lodged on the *primo piano*, as the Italians say, that is, on the second floor, of a large building in Fratina. In front of the windows of the first floor (*parterre*), in every Italian town, there are iron bars, and these Giuseppe Mansana grasped, swung himself up, and soon stood on the balcony outside of the Hungarian's chamber. He broke in the panes of the balcony window, opened it and disappeared. There was a light struck within — this his comrades who stood below saw. What else transpired they could not ascertain; they heard no noise, and Mansana has never told them. But after the lapse of a few minutes he and the Hungarian, the latter in his shirt, came out on the balcony, whereupon the Hungarian declared, in good French, that he had been drunk that evening, and begged pardon for what he had said; of course an Italian was just as good as a Hungarian. Mansana came down again the same way he had gone up.

Greater and lesser anecdotes from war times, from garrison and social life (among these some stories of racing which testified of an endurance in running I have never heard equaled), fell like hail upon us; but all that was told presents, it seems to me, the picture of a man whose presence of mind, courage, love of honor, whose physical strength and energy, dexterity and shrewdness, rouse to the highest pitch our expectations as to his future possibilities, but at the same time fill us with solicitude.

How Giuseppe Mansana came the following winter and spring to engross the attention of thousands, and among them the author of this volume, will appear in the story itself.

CHAPTER III.

WHEN Giuseppe Mansana followed his father's bones to their honored grave, looking as though he would like to leap over the hearse, he was — it soon became manifest — under the influence of a first passionate love. That same evening he took the railway train for Ancona, where his regiment was stationed. It was there she lived, the mere sight of whom had power to subdue the flames which burned with such consuming force.

He was in love with one who had his nature, one who must be conquered, one who had taken captive hundreds without being herself captured, one of whom an enamored Ancona bard had sung —

> Thou dusky devil, I do love thee,
> Thy smile of fire, thy blood of wine,
> And think it is the glow of evil
> Makes beauty in thy courage shine.
> Nay, think, the play which never ceases
> Of lustre in your face and eyes
> Is Satan's unrest in your nature,
> Your winning laughter his outvies.
> I think so, fair one! — but much rather
> I thee would love 'mid death and tears,
> Than fall asleep in arms that carry
> Me to the grave for fifty years.
> Yea, rather, much the queen of living
> In majesty that ends no more,
> E'en though I sink before the riddle,
> Than follow what I know oefore.

She was the daughter of an Austrian general and a lady who belonged to one of the oldest families in Ancona. It caused much indignation in its day that a woman of her rank should marry the commander of the detested foreign garrison.

The indignation was, if possible, increased by the fact that *he* was almost an old man, while *she* was but eighteen years of age and very beautiful. But the general's immense fortune might have tempted her; for she lived ir her splendid palace in actual poverty, — a matter of common occurrence in Italy. The fact is, the family palace is usually entailed property which the occupant is often unable to keep in repair. This was very nearly the case in the present instance. There might, however, have been some other attraction besides the general's wealth, for when, shortly after their daughter's birth, he died, the widow passed her period of mourning in absolute retirement. The church and the priest alone saw her. Friends, with whom she had broken at the time of her marriage, yet who now put themselves to all sorts of trouble in their efforts to again approach the enormously wealthy widow, she fled from.

Ancona, meanwhile, became Italian, and from the festivals, illuminations, and rejoicings she fled still farther, namely, to Rome, while her palace in Ancona, as well as her villa by the sea, remained closed and deserted as a mute protest. But in Rome, Princess Leaney discarded the black veil, without which no one had seen her since her husband's death, opened her salon, in which might be seen all the highest aristocracy of the papal dominion, and annually contributed large sums to the Peter-pence fund and other papal objects. The first as well as the last increased the hatred felt for her in Ancona, and which through the liberal party was also transported to Rome; and even on Monte Pincio, when, in all her beauty and splendor, she drove out with her little daughter, she could detect it in the glances flashed on her by familiar faces from Ancona and unfamiliar ones from Rome. She defied it, and not only regularly made her appearance on Monte Pincio, but also repaired anew to Ancona when summer drove her away from Rome. Once more she opened her Ancona palace and her villa, and passed most of the time in the latter place in order to avail herself of the baths. She made a point of driving through the town to her house on the Corso or to the church without greeting any one or being greeted in return, but nevertheless she repeated the trip every day. When her daughter grew larger, she allowed her to take part in the evening entertainments of plays and tableaux, which the priests of the city, under the protection of the bishop, got up for the benefit of the Peter-pence fund in Ancona; and so great was the child's beauty and the mother's attractiveness that many attended who would not otherwise have been willing to go. Thus the daughter learned defiance of the mother; and when at fourteen years of age the young girl lost her mother, she persevered in it on her own account, and with such additions as youth and courage involuntarily supply.

She was soon more talked about and more severely censured than her mother had ever been, inasmuch as her renown was more widely spread. For with an older lady, whom she took as a companion, a dignified, elegant person, who saw everything but spoke of nothing, she roamed through other countries, from England to Egypt, so planning her journeys, however, that she always passed her summers in Ancona, her autumns in Rome.

The last-named city became Italian finally, as well as Ancona; but in both cities she continued to lead what might be called a challenging life in the face of those who *now* ruled, and who sought in every way to win the rich, handsome woman. Indeed, it has been asserted that young noblemen formed alliances to conquer or crush her. Be this true or not, she believed it herself. And so she lured into her presence those whom she suspected, only to repulse them mercilessly. She first made them mad with hope, then with disappointment. She drove her horses herself through the Corso and on Monte Pincio; she appeared as a victor on a triumphal progress, with those she had vanquished bound to her carriage: not every one, to be sure, could see this, but *she* saw it because she felt it, and her victims felt it too.

She would have been slain, or even worse, had she not had too many worshipers, who in spite of everything formed a body-guard of perpetual adoration about her. To these belonged the bard before mentioned.

Above all else she became the secret hope and the open hatred of the young officers of the Ancona garrison.

Just at the time when Giuseppe Mansana had been removed with his Bersagliers to Ancona, she had been exercising a new caprice in that place. She had resolutely refused to adorn the company that assembled of evenings on the Corso, in order to promenade up and down, by the light of the moon, stars, and gas, the ladies in ball costume, holding before their faces the fans they can use with such wondrous effect, the gentlemen swarming around in fine new summer suits, or in their uniforms, meeting friends and acquaintances, laughing, gathering together about tables, where groups were already seated enjoying ices and coffee, then passing from these to others, finally to drop down at one themselves, while a quartet, or a wandering chorus, with cithern, flute, and guitar might be heard — Theresa Leaney res olutely refused to contribute to the splendor, the curiosity, the enjoyment, the nobility of these daily exhibitions of the town; on the contrary, she had chosen to be the cause of disturbance.

At sunset, when the carriages of other wealthy people were returning home, she drove out. With two unusually small ponies, the "Corsicans," by name, which she had that summer purchased, and, as was her wont, herself holding the reins, she would drive through the town in full trot. Then when the Corso was lighted and the rendezvous had begun, — the general rendezvous between families and friends, the clandestine one between young maidens and their adorers, the silent one between the idler and his shadow, the sighing one between the far-off betrothed lover and his faithful damsel here present, the brief one between the officer and his creditor, the excessively courteous one between the official and him whose death will give him a higher post, — just as the young ladies had succeeded in twice displaying their new Parisian dresses, that is to say, in one promenade up and one down the street, and the admiring store clerks had passed through the preliminaries, and the officers had formed their first critical group, and the nobility had just condescended to notice attentions, — this arrogant young girl, with her rigid, elderly companion at her side, would come dashing full speed into the midst of the group. The two little ponies would be in full trot, and the officers and young ladies, the nobility and the store clerks, family groups and whispering couples, must part in the utmost haste, in order to escape being run over. A row of bells on the harness of the ponies gave due warning, it was true, so that the police could say nothing; but all the more did those have to say whom she had insulted twofold: first by her absence, and then by her presence.

Two evenings Giuseppe Mansana had been on the Corso, and both times had come near being run over. He never before conceived the possibility of such assurance. He learned, too, who she was.

The third evening, when Theresa Leaney stopped at the accustomed place outside of the town, on her return trip, to have her ponies watered and allow them to rest before beginning their trot to the town and its Corso, a tall man stepped forward and saluted her. He was an officer.

"I take the liberty," said he, "of introducing myself. I am Giuseppe Mansana, officer of the Bersagliers. I have laid a wager to run a race with your little ponies from here to town. Have you any objections?"

It was after dusk, so that under ordinary circumstances she would not have been able to see him; but a strong excitement will sometimes increase our powers of vision. Astonishment, combined with a trifling degree of alarm — for there was something in the voice and bearing that startled her — gave her courage; for we often become courageous through fear. And so turning toward the small head and short face, of which she caught a faint glimpse, she said, —

"It occurs to me that a *gentleman* would have asked my permission before entering into such a wager; but an Italian officer" —

She did not continue, for she grew frightened herself at what she was saying, and there arose an ominous silence, during which her uneasiness increased. At last, she heard from a voice whose tones were more hollow than ever (Mansana's voice always had a hollow sound), —

"The wager is entered into with myself alone, and, to speak frankly, I propose to make the attempt, whether you consent or not."

"What?" exclaimed she, seizing the reins, but at the same moment she uttered a shriek and her companion a still louder one, as both came near falling from the carriage; for with a long whip neither of them had until now perceived the officer gave the ponies a furious cut across the backs, so that with a plunge they darted forward. Two servants, who had been sitting behind, and who had started to their feet at a sign from their young mistress to come to her aid, were thrown to the ground. Neither of them took part in the drive that now began, and that was not so long as it was rich in incidents.

To Giuseppe Mansana's acquirements — and possibly it was the most practiced of these — belonged, as indicated before, the art of running. The little ponies were not so hard to keep pace with, especially at the outset, when they were vigorously held back and were therefore not quite sure whether they should trot or not. Theresa, in her wrath, was ready to venture everything rather than tolerate such humiliation. She was determined, therefore, to give her servants time to catch up to her. But just as she was about to succeed in bringing the ponies to a halt, the lash fell whizzing on their backs and forthwith they darted off again. She said not a word, but drew in the reins again, and that so persistently that the ponies were about to halt once more; but then the whip fell anew, and again and yet again. And now she and they gave it up. Her elderly companion, who the whole time had shrieked and clung with both arms to Princess Leaney's waist, fell into a swoon, and had to be supported. Anger and dismay overwhelmed Theresa; for a while she saw neither ponies nor road, and at last she did not so much as know whether she held the reins. She had indeed dropped them but found them again in her lap, and made a second trial, holding her companion with one arm, yet at the same time managing to grasp the reins with both hands, striving with all her might to gain control of the terrified little ponies. She soon realized the impossibility of this. It was dark; the tall poplars trotted with them in the air step by step, above the brushwood that grew between them. She knew not where she was. The sole object she could distinguish besides the ponies was the tall form by their side, that like a spectre towered above them, always at the same height and the same distance. Where were they going? And swift as lightning it flashed through her mind: "Not to the town; he is no officer, he is a bandit; I am being driven away from the road — soon others will join him!" And from the depths of the anguish caused by this sudden idea, she screamed, —

"Stop, for Heaven's sake! What do you want? Do you not see" —

She got no farther, for she heard a whizzing sound in the air, the whip cracked on the backs of the ponies, and harder than ever the little animals dashed onward.

Swift as the speed of the ponies was the flight of her thoughts. "What does he want? Who is he? One of those whom I have insulted?" And in rapid succession the ranks of these passed in review before her. She could find no one whom he seemed to resemble. But the thought of vengeance pursued her startled conscience; it might indeed be one whom she did not know, but who wanted to take revenge for all the others. But if this was revenge, she had yet the worst to expect. The bells cut through the rattling of the carriage-wheels; the short, sharp sound darted about her like shrieks of anguish, and, roused to the utmost by terror, she was ready to risk a leap from the carriage. But no sooner had she relaxed her hold on her companion than the latter rolled over like a lifeless object, and in greater terror than ever the princess picked her up, and with the rigid form thrown across her lap sat a long time devoid of a single clear idea. At last, as the road made a sudden turn, she perceived a luminous haze over the town. She felt the joy of deliverance, but only for a moment, brief as a glance, for the next instant she comprehended the whole : he was an avenger from the Corso !

"Oh, no farther!" exclaimed she, even before the thought was fully matured. "Oh, no ! "

The words echoed in her ears, the bells leaped with shrill intonation about the group, the poplars trotted alongside, but that was all : the race went on, but there came no answer. She saw in her mind's eye her pitiful progress through the city, lashed forward with her fainting companion in her arms, and the public on either side, with the officers foremost applauding and jeering. For this was the officers' revenge ; she was sure of it now. She bowed her head as if she were already there. Then she felt and heard that the ponies were slackening their speed ; they must be near their destination ; but would they pause before they got there? Once more, with a sudden hope, she looked up. He had dropped behind, — that was the cause of this respite. He was close by her side ; soon she heard his hasty, labored breathing, heard finally nothing else, until all her anxiety became centred in the thought, " What if he should fall in the middle of the Corso, with blood streaming from his lips and nostrils!" His blood would then be on her head; for her challenging defiance had called forth his. The people would spring upon her and tear her to pieces.

"Spare yourself!" she begged. "I will yield!" she cried, in tones of agonized entreaty.

But as though startled out of his artful experiment, he made one final effort, and in two or three longer strides was once more abreast with the ponies, who the moment they became conscious of his presence, accelerated their speed, but received, nevertheless, two whizzing lash strokes.

Now she distinctly saw the first gas-lights near the Cavour monument; soon they would turn into the Corso; the play was about to begin. She felt an unconquerable desire to weep, and yet could not shed a tear, and then she bowed her head in order to shut out all further sight. At that moment she heard the sound of his voice, but not what he said; the carriage was now on the paving-stones, and besides, he was most likely unable to speak distinctly. She looked up again, but he was no longer visible. Great God! had he fallen to the ground? Every drop of blood stood still within her veins. No: there he was, walking slowly away from the Corso, past the Café Garibaldi. At the same moment she found herself in the Corso; the horses trotted, the people cleared the way; she bowed her head still lower over the fainting companion lying across her lap; terror and shame were chasing after them with the lash.

When some moments later she came to a halt in the palace court-yard, through whose open gate the ponies had rushed full speed, so that it was a miracle the carriage was not upset or dashed to pieces, — she too fainted.

An old servant stood awaiting her coming. He called for help; the two ladies were borne into the palace. Shortly afterward the men who had been thrown from the carriage made their appearance, and related what had occurred, so far as they knew it. The old servant took them soundly to task for their awkwardness, so that they actually felt ashamed of it themselves and all the more readily did as he bade them: maintained a discreet silence.

The ponies had run away just as the servants, after a short rest, were about mounting the box. That was all.

CHAPTER IV.

When Princess Theresa Leaney awoke to consciousness her strength seemed wholly exhausted. She did not rise from her couch, she scarcely ate a morsel; no one was allowed to remain with her.

Her companion walked noiselessly through the great mirrored hall opposite the ante-room, and noiselessly back again when she had finished her errands. Just as noiselessly she stepped back into the small gothic chamber occupied by the princess. The servants followed her example. Princess Leaney's companion had been brought up in a convent, had come forth from there with high pretensions on the score of her rank and her acquirements, pretensions she maintained for ten years and then for five more — constantly outraged by the inelegance and greed of youth. Finally she obtained in an aristocratic family a position befitting a lady of rank, still silently preserving her feeling of injured dignity; but as she grew older she submitted to one thing after another, without, however, losing her sense of affront; she held her peace about everything and devoted all her energies to the accumulation of wealth. Her great secret of success lay in making herself thoroughly acquainted with all that concerned her lofty patrons, and in using her knowledge to the profit of *both* parties.

And so she was silent. After the lapse of a few days there came from the gothic chamber of the princess the curt little command: " Pack up!" From later bulletins it was ascertained that a very long journey was in prospect. In a few days more the princess came forth herself, walked about slowly and silently, gave orders concerning some trifles and wrote some letters. After this she disappeared again. The next day brought the message: " This evening at seven o'clock." At the stroke of six she appeared herself in traveling costume, accompanied by her maid, who was also dressed for traveling. The companion stood ready for departure beside the trunks which the servant, who was all ready too, was to close, after the princess had cast an approving glance at their contents.

The first word the companion had spoken to Princess Leaney since their memorable drive she now uttered. As though by chance she placed herself at the side of the princess, and looking out into the court-yard softly observed:

"People in town only know that our ponies ran away — nothing more."

A withering look of displeasure met her gaze; this was gradually transformed into one of astonishment, and this in turn into one of dismay.

"Is he then dead?" the princess gasped, and every word quivered with agonized dread.

"No, I saw him an hour since."

The companion did not return the look the princess gave her, nor had she done so before; she was gazing out into the court-yard toward the stable, from which the carriage had been drawn out and the horses just led forward. When finally she found it advisable to turn, — and it was long before she did find this advisable, as the princess said nothing and the servant did not stir; he must have seen something before him which riveted him to the spot, — when finally the companion deemed it advisable to turn she saw in the twinkling of an eye that the effect of her information had been complete. The terrified imagination of the princess had naturally, during these feverish days, pictured the jubilant derision which must now fill the town; she had fancied it spreading as far as Rome, indeed, through the newspapers, over the whole world; she had felt her hitherto un bowed, brilliant defiance annihilated in a few hideous moments; it had seemed to her as if she had been dragged through the mire by the hair of her head. And so no one besides him and themselves knew what had occurred? He had kept perfectly silent? What a man!

The beautiful large eyes of the princess darted flashes of fire around the room, but shortly afterward they assumed a laughing radiance; she drew up her head and her whole figure, took several turns up and down the room, as far as the trunks and other traveling luggage permitted, then smiling and giving her parasol a little twirl, she said, —

"Unpack! We will not go to-day!"

Then she abruptly left the room.

In a short time the maid came and asked the companion to dress for a walk.

As often and as long as they had been in Ancona it was the first time the princess had been willing to take part in the evening promenade of the fashionable world. Therefore the companion would have had opportunity for some astonished words in reply to the look of astonishment with which the maid accompanied this announcement; but the look was in itself an impertinence, and so there was nothing said. When Theresa, all dressed, entered the great mirror-lined, pillared salon, she could see through the open door into the faintly-lighted ante-room, and there she beheld her companion standing waiting. The costume of the princess alone would have justified the maid's expression of countenance as she opened and closed the door; but the companion followed as though they had been every day accustomed to make this expedition and as though the princess appeared every evening in such elegant attire.

In a lilac silk dress, richly trimmed with lace, she rustled down the steps. Her figure was vigorous and already rather full, and yet it gave an impression of suppleness because she was also tall and had a certain vivacious bearing. Contrary to her custom she now wore her hair dressed in braids, and there floated behind her a long lace veil, fastened on one side of the head with a brooch, on the other with a rose; the sleeves of her dress were so open that when she used her fan, her long gloves did not quite suffice to cover her arms. She did not join her companion, but strode briskly forward; it was the duty of the other to keep always at her side.

The evening was lively, for there was pleasant weather for the first time after some blustering days. But as the princess advanced al-

conversation stopped only to begin again, when she had passed, with a tumultuous current, like a stream that had been dammed up and let loose again. Princess Theresa Leaney participating in the evening promenade! Princess Theresa Leaney on the Corso! And *how?* Radiant with beauty, wealth, graciousness, with a friendly look for all, she saluted the ladies she had been in the habit of seeing from childhood up, the merchants she had dealt with, the noblemen and officers she had conversed with. In this the most renowned of all Italian towns for the beauty of its women, she did not, to be sure, carry off the palm; nevertheless, far and near she had been surnamed " the beauty from Ancona," and the town had for many years been ready to lower its banner and join in the anthem of homage whenever she wished. And now she was willing. There was a look of insinuating entreaty in the eyes with which she smiled a greeting on her " people," something apologetic in the bow with which the smile was accompanied. As she returned she remarked the change in the sentiments of her subjects, and ventured to pause and converse with the members of one of the oldest noble families of the town. They were sitting in front of a café in the middle of the Corso. They received her with surprise, yet courteously; she cared for the rest herself. The old gentleman, who was the head of the family, became more and more fascinated the longer she remained, and took pride and delight in presenting every one to her. She had a friendly greeting for all, was witty, joyous, and divided her attentions equally between the ladies and the gentlemen, until an atmosphere was created that finally became laden with merriment. The group kept constantly increasing in size, and when she moved away a large triumphal procession and loud-voiced conversation accompanied her. It might be said that the Corso was that evening the scene of a festival of universal reconciliation between the best society of the town and this its comely child, and it seemed as though both parties were alike happy therein.

The evening was advancing when she, and her followers with her, rose once more from champagne and ices; it was for the third time. She found no rest very long in any one place. Gayly but slowly the party moved on up the street. Three officers came walking along, somewhat covered with dust, and with rapid steps; they were evidently returning from a long expedition. The companion found her way, as by chance, to the side of the princess and whispered something in her ear. The princess looked up, and at once recognized the form — there came Mansana!

Quite as a matter of course the companion then glided over to the other side, and Theresa moved farther along toward the place she had left; it was so near the officers that the nearest one could have stroked her dress with his sabre had he chosen to come one step closer. Now the nearest one was Mansana. The princess saw that he recognized her; the light fell full on the spot. She observed that he was surprised. But she also noticed that the short vigorous face seemed, as it were, to close itself, that the small deep eyes at once became veiled. He had the considerate tact not to appear to recognize her. She gave him a look for *that* and for his silence, besides — her large dark eyes sparkled, — a look that went to his heart and kindled there a fire that burst in flames over his cheeks. He walked on, no longer able to fix his thoughts on the conversation of his comrades. He was obliged, too, to take the express train early that night in order to follow his father's bones, the next day, to their grave of honor in his native place. No one deemed it singular that he went home early.

CHAPTER V

THE next day, as we have before seen, he followed his father's bier with a desire, seemingly, to leap far over and beyond it. That one look bestowed on *him*, who had insulted her, by Princess Theresa Leaney, in whom he, in his proud defiance, had expected to find a deadly enemy, that one look from out of all her beauty and in the midst of her triumphal progress on the Corso, had created a new image, and placed it on a pedestal within his soul. It was the image of the princess herself, as life's own victory-radiant goddess. Before this pure, sublime beauty, all calumny sank away as the feeble, vain efforts of a petty soul, and his own conduct seemed like a presumptuous, contemptible piece of brutality. Was it *she* he had dared frighten and pursue?

And the development that had led him to such profanation, that is to say, his own hard life experience, he now tore asunder, link by link, as he followed his father's bier, beginning with his father himself. For from his father this dangerous inheritance of defiance had been transmitted to his soul, where it had taken root. It had inspired him with an egotistic, savage will; he had most truly been his own model in every respect. Had his father been anything very different?

His noble and beautiful mother had so often wept as she sat alone with her children; her tears were an accusation against the man who had forsaken wife, child, and property to follow — what? — his defiance, his ambition, his revenge, which so often are the unruly comrades of patriotism, becoming at last its masters. He knew this to be so from his own experience and from that of hundreds of others who were now passed in review, one by one.

The music pealed forth, the cannons roared, the air was filled with cries of *Evviva* and flowers in honor of his father's memory.

"What hollowness in such a life," thought the son: "from conspiracy to prison, from prison to conspiracy again, while mother, wife, and child tread the path to poverty; while property is sold and nothing gained except the restless heart's rapid flight from suffering in revenge to revenge in suffering again. And this suffering was the inheritance of my childhood — and with it an empty life!"

And his father's old friends gathered about him to press his hand. They congratulated him on his father's honor, they even congratulated him on being the worthy heir.

"Aye, my life has been as hollow as his," he continued in his thoughts. "Swayed by a delight in revenge, as long as there was war, a restless craving for adventure of necessity followed, a vain ambition, a conceited sense of invincibility became the controlling element of life — brutal, selfish, hollow, all of it." And he vowed that henceforth his comrades should have something else to talk about than Giuseppe Mansana's last exploit, and that he himself would strive for a nobler pride than that caused by being sated with the consciousness that *he* never spoke of himself.

The nearer they drew to Mansana's birthplace, the more exultant became the throng and the more eager to see Giuseppe, the martyr's celebrated son. But to him, here on the play-grounds of his childhood, it seemed as if his grandmother once more sat on the curb-stone and was now casting stones at the procession: she was stoning that which had trampled under foot her life with all that she had gathered about her to make it happy.

Yet when his mother's grave, troubled eye rested on him, her gaze seemed almost an insult. *She* did not know what thoughts he had just been cherishing about all this, and about his own life as a continuation of his father's.

Why should she give him so anxious a look, when he had just bidden farewell to the temptations of a passion for honor? And he returned her gaze defiantly, for it did not strike home to him.

CHAPTER VI.

Two days later Mansana stood on the heights by the wall surrounding the ancient cathedral of Ancona. Neither on the noseless red marble lions that are the bearers of the porch pillars, nor on the glorious bay lying at his feet, did he bestow a look. His eye, indeed, glided over the decks of the ships and boats of lading below, as well as over the busy life in the arsenals and about the wharves; but his thoughts still lingered in the cathedral where he had just been himself, for there he had seen *her*. A solemn festival had called her thither. He had seen her kneel, and what was more, she had seen him! Aye, she had evidently been glad to see him, and had given him the same indescribable look as on that ever memorable evening. He could not gaze at her any longer without being obtrusive or attracting attention, and, besides, the incense-laden air and the dim, religious light had become unbearable to him. Here, though, it was fresh and free, and thoughts of beautiful objects could float about amid the beauty of the surrounding scene. Behind him he heard the people leaving the church; he saw them again in the windings of the road below, on foot and in carriages: he would not glance round, he was waiting until he could see *her* below him. Suddenly he heard steps approaching of one, of two persons; his heart throbbed, a mist gathered before his eyes; for the whole world he would not have turned. Some one paused at his side, also in front of the wall. He felt who it was and could not refrain from turning without appearing discourteous. She, too, was now gazing out over the ships, the bay, and the sea, but observed at once that he had changed his position. Her face was flushed, but she colored still more deeply as she smiled and said, —

"Pardon me for seizing this opportunity. I saw you, and I *must* express my thanks."

She ceased. She wanted to say more, he was sure of that. It did not come at once, it was quite an eternity before it came. But at last he heard the words :-

"There are times when nothing could be more magnanimous than silence. Thank you!"

She bowed forward, and he again ventured to look up. What grace! What a smile was hers, as she glided away, followed by her companion! What a walk, what a noble form! And her long veil floated about in the wind, playing against her red velvet dress.

The road leading down from the heights is a winding one; her carriage, which had halted at some distance, now drove up toward her and turned below the upper wall. But she had not reached it before she too heard footsteps behind her, almost running steps; she stood still and looked round; she knew who it was. She met his impetuosity with a smile, doubtless to set him at his ease.

"I did not at once fully comprehend," said he, as he bowed to her, while a deep flush overspread his bronzed face. "But it was by no means out of consideration that I was silent, it was from pride. I will not appropriate an honor I do not in the least deserve. And pardon me for my rudeness."

There was a tremor in his deep-toned voice; he spoke with an effort· Mansana was not a man of words. As he touched his hat, however, to make his parting salutation, his hand trem bled, and this, as well as what had gone before, gave the princess an impression of great eloquence.

And thus it came to pass that Princess Theresa was attracted by so much frankness, and felt a desire to reward it; for what discoveries had not she also made about herself. And thus it happened, furthermore, that Princess Theresa did not step into her carriage, but walked past it between Captain Mansana and her companion. Thus also it chanced that she retraced her steps at his side, and that for more than an hour they walked back and forth at the foot of the upper wall, with the glorious view below them.

And when finally after she had taken her seat in the carriage and was being whirled round the curve leading into the lower road that ran parallel with the one she had just left, she once more sent him a bow and a smile in response to his renewed salutation, — he continued his march to and fro in the same spot for another hour. The sharp outlines of the bay, the verdure-clad slope of the mountains, the blue infinity of the sea, the sails dotted over the latter, and the columns of smoke in the horizon, — beautiful indeed is the bay of Ancona!

Through this unpremeditated encounter she

had gained about the same knowledge that he had gained; the history of her past had been very similar to that of his; she had told him so in acknowledging her vain defiance, her struggling ambition: with suppressed exultation, he had received this confession, word by word, from her lips.

Yonder image of beauty, far, far beyond *his* plane of existence, *now* hovered smiling about him, full of faults and yearnings like his own, but encircled by a halo of loveliness and glory into which he felt himself uplifted.

Oh, the Bay of Ancona! how bold its windings, how keenly blue-black the bosom of its waters in a breeze, how soft the transitions of color out upon the sea, terminating in a luminous haze!

CHAPTER VII.

WHAT was it that prevented him from presenting himself forthwith at her palace? A secret hope that she might once more appear to him. A vanity as long buried within the heart and nurtured in secret as Mansana's had been, is capable of the most astonishing surprises; it can, in fact, be both shy and daring at the same time. He was really too shy to seek her, notwithstanding her invitation; and yet he was bold enough to believe that she would herself come to the place where she had last met him. He went every day to mass, but she did not come; and when he met her accidentally by the sea, and on foot, he saw that she was either embarrassed or displeased at his non-appearance, he could not understand which.

Too late he discovered that in cherishing a hope founded on his vanity, he had set aside all common politeness. He hastened to the palace and sent in his card.

An old Italian palace which often has a foundation wall built in the days of the great empire, an interior dating back to the Middle Ages or transition period, an exterior with façade and portico from the days of the renaissance, or a period directly following, and whose ornamentations and furniture belong to quite as many ages, while the statues, carvings, movables, may be traced back, the first to the plunderings of the Crusaders in the Greek islands and in Constantinople, the rest to the Byzantine period, and thence carried down to the present day, — such an Italian palace, which can only be found in seaport towns, is a fragment of the history of civilization as well as that of a family; and it produces a strong impression on him who enters it, especially if he be one who was born among the people and is endowed with keen powers of observation. It also invests her who is established therein as the mistress of the triumphal hall of her ancestors, with a consciousness which imparts to friendliness something condescending, to politeness something aristocratic; but even this is not needed to remove her to a great distance from one who approaches her with an evil conscience. The surroundings in such an instance have a terribly subduing effect: even the familiar intercourse of a few preceding interviews cannot prevent the grand stairways, the lofty apartments, the history of a thousand years, from intimidating one who passes through the portal with a breach of courtesy on his conscience. If in addition to all this one's imagination has pictured somewhat closer relations with the mistress of the palace, that same imagination will frighten one away to a greater distance than needful.

Thus it came to pass that the first meeting proved a failure. Mansana was invited to call again, and did so with the embarassing sense that the previous interview had been awkward; consequently the second call turned out badly.

Afterward he met the princess with his wounded vanity on guard — and saw her smile.

All his proud defiance then returned. But what could he do? Here he dared not swear, not even speak; he was silent; he suffered, he went away, came again, and became aware that she was toying with his agony! Had she once felt herself vanquished, she now learned the relish of conquering her victor: she was treading familiar paths, and thus she bore herself with entrancing superiority.

Never did captured lion so tug at his chains as did Giuseppe Mansana at the delicate network of ceremonials and patronizing condescension that surrounded him. Nevertheless, it was impossible for him to remain away. In the frenzy of his nights and the soul-consuming mad chase, round and round in the same circle, by day, his strength was exhausted. Humility took possession of him.

He could not bear to hear her discussed by others; and he himself dared not mention her name lest he should betray his passion and become an object of derision. He could not brook seeing her in the society of others; and he himself dared not associate with her lest he should be compelled to undergo some humiliation Not once, but a hundred times he felt a desire to slay both her and whoever for the moment she preferred to him, but was forced to control himself and go away. He was thoroughly convinced that this must lead to insanity or death, perhaps to both.

Yet so utterly powerless was he to struggle against his danger that at times he would lie flat on the ground in order to present to himself a picture of his own utter helplessness.

Why not end his career in some deed, some brilliant deed of revenge, worthy of his past? But, like thunder-clouds above a mountain, thoughts like these glided across his soul while it was in the fetters of Nature's law.

At last he was formally bidden to Princess Theresa's palace. One of the most celebrated musicians of Europe, returning that autumn from still farther south, passed through Ancona, and stopped there to pay his respects to the princess, whose acquaintance he had made in Vienna. She invited all the *élite* of Ancona to a superb festival, the first she had given in her palace. The arrangements were worthy of her wealth and station; universal joy prevailed, bearing along in the current the invalid master himself, who took a seat at the piano and began to play. The first note he struck had power to transform the entire assemblage into a group of friends, as often happens when beauty removes all restraints.

Theresa's eyes sought those of others, in order that she, too, might give and receive; and as her gaze wandered around it fell on Mansana, who in complete self-forgetfulness had pressed forward and was standing close beside the piano. The master was playing a composition entitled "Longing," in which out of the most profound anguish there was a reaching upward for consolation. He played like one who had known sorrow that bore him to the brink of despair. Never had the princess beheld a countenance like Mansana's at this moment. It was harder than usual, aye repulsively hard; and yet tear after tear rolled in rapid succession down his cheeks. He looked as if he were bracing himself with an iron will, in order not to break down, and at the same time he gave the impression of trying to force back his tears. She had never seen anything so full of contradiction and so wretched. She gazed intently at him, and becoming overwhelmed at last by a strange dizziness that even caused her to believe that it was he who was in danger of falling, she rose to her feet. A loud burst of applause brought her to her senses, at the same moment so far withdrawing all eyes from her that she gained time to compose herself and wait until she could again safely dare to look up and endeavor to draw a long breath.

The composition was not quite ended, but she saw Mansana steal toward a door; doubtless the applause had startled him, too, and led him to the discovery that he was unable to control his emotions.

Her terror of a moment since still tingling through her veins, she abruptly sped through the listening multitude, to the astonishment of all, and passing out of the nearest door, hastened onward as though it depended on her to hinder a misfortune, — not without a feeling of guilt, not without a feeling of responsibility. As she had expected, he stood in the ante-room, where he had just thrown his cloak over his shoulders; his hat was already on his head. None of the servants were at hand, for they too had taken the liberty to listen to the music, and so she walked rapidly forward.

"Signore!"

He turned, met her flashing eyes, and saw her excitement, as with both hands she stroked back the stray locks from cheeks and neck, a movement which with her always betokened decision but at the same time invested her form with its highest beauty.

"The train yesterday brought me the new Hungarian horses I told you about lately. To-morrow we must try them. Pray, will not you do me the kindness to drive for me? Will you not?"

His bronzed skin grew pale; she heard his rapid breathing. But he neither looked up nor spoke, he merely bowed in acquiescence. Then he laid his hand on the artistically wrought door handle, which yielded with a sonorous sound.

"At four o'clock," she added, hurriedly.

He bowed once more without raising his eyes, but in the open door he turned toward her again, hat in hand, proudly erect. This was his farewell. He saw her bestow on him a questioning look. *His* countenance might have called this forth. It certainly could not have concealed the flash of inspiration which illumined his gloomy mind, for now the knowledge had come to him how all this was to end.

CHAPTER VIII.

At four o'clock the next day he was ushered by a servant through the ante-room and mirrored salon into the concert hall, and onward to one of the interior gothic rooms, where lay scattered the photographs of the last journey. It was announced to him that the princess would be ready immediately.

She made her appearance in a sort of Hungarian or Polish costume; the weather was rather chilly now in November, and especially to-day. She wore a close-fitting velvet dress, with a sable-edged sacque, which reached to the knees, on her head was a high, sable-trimmed cap, her hair floated loose.

As she gave him her hand, which was cased in a white glove, whose sable heading was bordered with lace, it was with the same firm, confiding trust to which eyes, face, aye, the voluptuous form itself, bore witness. *It could not be otherwise!* At all events, *his* interpretation was that she wanted to manifest a confidence she did not possess. This was confirmed by her soon lightly observing that perhaps it might be as well to postpone the drive: the horses had not yet recovered from the shock of their railroad travel. With cold derision he dismissed her fears. She studied his face: it betokened excitement and suffering, but was otherwise a closed book — as it was wonderfully capable of appearing. His manner was distant but more decided than it had been for a long time. Word was brought that the horses were waiting without; at the same moment the companion entered. Mansana offered the princess his arm; she took it. On the steps she again looked up in his face and thought she perceived a light in it. Now she was alarmed. At the carriage door, availing herself of the opportunity arising from the necessity of having the horses held while they got into the vehicle, she again said, —

" Is it not really too soon to drive with them ? Had we not better put it off until another time ? "

Her voice quivered as she spoke, and laying her trembling hand on Mansana's arm, she looked up trustingly into his eyes. His countenance became transformed under this look, his eyes darkened.

" I thought you would scarcely be willing to venture on a drive with me — a second time ! "

Blushing crimson, the princess jumped into the carriage. Pale as a corpse, rigid as a pole the companion followed; but as though bound for the dance Mansana sprang lightly on the box. No servant accompanied them, the carriage was a light one-seated vehicle.

As soon as the horses were set free, the danger became manifest; the animals stood on their hind legs, one of them pulled in one direction, one in another. It certainly took more than a minute to drive through the gate. "Good Heavens! to think that you should wish this!" whispered the companion, her eyes fixed in deadly terror on the two animals, who reared and plunged and reared again, received each a blow with the whip, darted back, tried to spring to one side, received another blow, drew back, gained another blow, and finally started forward. The mode of applying the lash was evidently not the most approved in the world.

When the street was reached the two foreign horses began to tremble and stamp on the ground; the new objects about them, the new sounds, the new coloring, the brilliant southern light and warm glow over everything, frightened them. But Mansana's skill and strength of arms kept them in a gentle walk until they had passed the Cavour monument; then they began gradually to break loose. Mansana looked over his shoulder and met Princess

Theresa's eyes, and now it was he who was happy and she who suffered.

What could have led her to the unlucky notion of planning this drive? No sooner had she proposed it than she regretted having done so. She had felt sure, the moment she detected that gleam in his eye yesterday, that he would use this drive as a punishment, and that too with the same merciless resolution he had shown before. Why, then, was she sitting here? While noting accurately every movement made by him, by the horses, she asked herself this question over and over again, not with a view of obtaining an answer, but because her thoughts *must* be active.

Forward sped the horses in the most rapid trot that was possible; nor did their speed slacken. Mansana finally looked round. It was a movement of exultation; his eyes shot fire. But this was only the momentary introduction to what followed. Raising his whip, and giving it a dexterous swing, he let it fall whizzing on the backs of both animals at once. No sooner did they hear its sound in the air than with a leap forward they broke into a gallop.

Not a sound from the two who sat within.

Then he repeated the feat, thereby completely maddening the horses.

The road began to wind up a steeper and steeper hill. And just at this point Mansana raised the whip for the third time, swung it over his head like a lasso, and let it fall.

Now this action, during this furious speed, at such a place, was clear as a lightning flash in its significance: it was not punishment he sought, it was death, — death with her!

If there be any faculty of our soul which testifies of its divine origin it is this: the amount of time and number of events it can compass in the second of a second. From the moment when the whip inscribed that jubilant arc in the air until it fell, Princess Leaney had not only discovered but had actually experienced their united lives, interpreted by the new light, and had gained certainty in regard to this silent, proud love of Mansana's, that made him ready to meet death with exultation when it could be shared with her, — and in that same second of a second she had both formed her resolve and carried it into execution.

For simultaneously with the fall of the whip he heard behind him the one word, "Mansana!" — not uttered in terror or condemnation: no, it was a wild shout of joy. He whirled round; there, in the midst of this tempestuous drive, she stood erect, with beaming countenance and outstretched arms. More rapidly than it can be told, he had turned toward the horses, thrown aside the whip, wound the reins three times around his arms, and, straining every nerve, braced himself against the dash-board of the carriage. He would live with her.

Now, indeed, a desperate struggle ensued. He had resolved to turn the course of death's bridal procession into that of life.

In a whirling cloud of dust, on the very brink of the precipice, they dashed stormily onward; the foaming horses could be forced to hold their heads higher, so that their manes fluttered behind them, like sable pinions, — that was all. At last Mansana grasped the right rein with both hands, in order to guide the mad race into the middle of the road, — taking his chance about encountering whatever obstacle might be in the way; for at all events they should pass proudly through the portal of death. He succeeded in getting the horses into the middle of the road, but their speed was not checked, — and lo! far beyond he thought he descried a mass of objects approaching; the whole road was blocked up by it. A nearer view proved it to be one of those interminable herds of cattle which in the autumn are driven to the seashore.

Then he started to his feet, flinging the reins over the dash-board. A loud shriek behind him! He leaped forward; still another piercing shriek; but he was already on the back of the right horse, grasping the other by the bit. The one on which he was sitting sprang into the air while still running, whereby it was thrown down by the other horse. It was nevertheless carried along for some distance by the outer thill until this broke beneath the burden, and was then still dragged onward until the neck-yoke also gave way. Mansana's grasp of the bit saved him, and together with the weight of the disabled horse, brought the race to an end. But the fallen horse felt the carriage upon it and kicked out wildly; the one standing reared; the carriage pole snapped, one piece struck Mansana on the side, yet he did not relax his hold, and was now in front of, or rather under, the standing horse, with a cruel grip in its nostrils, until it became as meek as a captured, trembling lamb. He was up himself in a moment; the prostrate horse, which had made several dangerous attempts to rise, was helped.

And now, thickly covered with dust, tattered and torn, bleeding, hatless, Mansana for the first time ventured to look up and about him.

Theresa was standing at the open carriage door. She must have been about to jump out and have been cast back by one of the terrible shocks they had experienced, and have started to her feet again, — or something to that effect; she herself knew not how it had happened. But what she now did fully comprehend was that *he* stood there safe, holding the shivering horses by the bits.

Out of the carriage and toward him she sprang; and he turned to receive her with wide open arms; she flung herself into them! Bosom was strained to bosom, lip sought lip, and thus these lofty forms stood wrapped each in the other's embrace. And this seemed as though it would never end. The arms did not relax, not even to renew their clasp, neither were lips nor eyes withdrawn; hers only sank deeper into his.

The first word that was spoken was a whispered " Theresa ! " Then their lips were again sealed.

Never did woman with greater rejoicing accept the place of ruler than she that of subject when this embrace at last came to an end. Never did fugitive, with such prodigiously sparkling, joyous eyes, beg pardon for having struggled for freedom. Never before did princess plunge with such zeal into her duties as a slave, as did she, when she discovered his wound, his torn and dust-covered condition. With her delicate white hands and her rich handkerchief and pins, she began to cleanse, bind up, and fasten together, and with her eyes she healed and made whole, — perhaps not the wounds, and yet it really was the wounds, for he felt them no more.

For each little service, there was an added caress, fresh silent or spoken joy. Finally they so entirely forgot carriage, horses, and companion, that they betook themselves on their way toward town, as though there remained to them nothing more than to press onward with their new-found happiness. A cry of alarm from the companion and the slowly approaching herd awakened them.

CHAPTER IX.

THEIR blissful intoxication neither ended that day nor the days that immediately followed. The higher circles of Ancona were drawn into it, since the betrothal was celebrated with fêtes and excursions. There was indeed something startlingly romantic in the whole affair. Mansana's fame, the wealth, rank, and beauty of the princess; *she* the hitherto invincible, *he* the ever victorious; and then even the circumstances attending the betrothal, that in the mouths of the people had acquired the most incredible embellishments, — all this combined to heighten one degree Princess Theresa's felicity, surrounding it with a truly magic halo.

When these two were seen together, a fine contrast was presented by them. They were both tall, they had the same elastic step and proud carriage; but her face was long, his short; her eyes were large and wide-open, his small and deep. One could not but admire her delicate, long nose, pouting lips, noble chin, beautifully arched cheeks, encircled by black hair; but his low brow, small, firmly compressed mouth, defiant chin, shortly-cropped hair, did not invest him with beauty. Quite as great was the difference between her outwardly-manifested joy, her brilliant discourse, and his taciturn manner.

But neither she nor their friends would have had him otherwise, not even at such a time as this; for he was true to his nature. Why even matters on which he was ready to stake his life became transformed into every-day commonplaces when he allowed himself to talk about them; but as a rule he did not talk.

And so neither the princess nor the social circle in which she and Mansana moved, perceived that now, aye, at this very time, he was undergoing a great change.

There is a certain boundless submission, a jealous zeal in rendering service, which converts the recipient into a slave or a mere tool. Not a moment's liberty, not a particle of freedom of will is allowed to remain. The slightest expression of anything of the kind calls forth twenty new plans for the attainment of what is desired and a tumult of passionate actions.

There is a way of giving confidence which insinuates itself into those precincts of our soul where mortal has never penetrated before — divines thoughts, brings to light reflections, and is exceedingly embarrassing to one who has been in the habit of living shut up within himself.

Such and more was the case in regard to Mansana. Within a few days he was satiated; the ineffable exhaustion resulting from excitement, that of despair as well as that of joy, made him doubly irritable. There were moments when he abhorred the sight both of her and of society.

He was shocked himself at this as at the blackest ingratitude, and in the honesty of his soul he finally confessed it to her. He gave her some idea of what he had suffered, and how near destruction he had been, showing her that this excess of mad public festivity was just the opposite of what he needed. He could bear no more.

She was deeply moved by this revelation. In the midst of a cloud of the wildest self-accusations, she decided on rest for him, departure for herself. *She* would go to Rome and Hungary to make arrangements for the wedding; *he* should go to a mountain fortress farther south, where he could exchange with an officer who wanted to be in Ancona. She was so strong she speedily carried this plan into execution. Within two days both he and she had left the place. The parting on her side was very affecting; on his, truly heartfelt: her love and ardor touched him.

But no sooner was he alone, first on the journey and afterward in the garrison, than he sank into a state of complete apathy. He had scarcely any other recollection of her than a confused tumult of impressions. He could not even prevail on himself to open the letters that came from her; he shrank from her vehemence

The fact was she telegraphed and wrote at least once each day, and when his obligations to reply pressed too heavily upon him, he fled from his own room, where all lay unfulfilled and waiting. When not on duty, therefore, he wandered about in the woods and hills beyond the town, for the country was unusually wild and beautiful in this vicinity.

On these excursions he could dissolve all he had been through into a species of illusion. The title of principessa-eccellenza has not the same charm in Italy as elsewhere; there are too many who bear it, some of them occupying questionable positions. Nor had the fortune inherited by Theresa from her father anything alluring about it, for it had been gained by her mother through treachery to the fatherland in its period of degradation. Neither did Theresa's beauty continue to hold sway, for it was beginning to grow too ripe. Their romantic meeting no longer sufficed to wipe out the long humiliation she had at first permitted him to endure, and her final abandonment left behind a sense of *ennui*. In stronger moments, however, Mansana's dream-images strove to attain different forms, but then his pride revolted and assured him that in a union with Princess Leaney he must always be the inferior, perchance in the end the toy of her caprices. Had he not already been so?

After his morning walk he usually rested on a bench beneath an old olive-tree, just beyond the town. From there he walked down to his breakfast. One morning he saw two people, an elderly gentleman and a young lady, take their seats on the bench as he left it. The same thing occurred the next morning and at the same hour. The day following this he kept his seat rather longer than usual, not without design, and thus had an opportunity to look at the young lady and talk with the old gentleman. The facility with which Italians enter into a conversation and an acquaintance soon made him possessor of the facts that the gentleman was a pensioner from the past administration; that the young lady was his daughter, was about fifteen years of age, and was just out of a convent. She kept very close to her father and spoke but little, yet Mansana thought she had the sweetest voice he had ever heard.

Afterward they met every day and not by chance. He always waited on the heights until he saw them coming up from the town, and then he approached the bench. They were both very friendly and quiet. The old gentleman fel into the habit of talking a little every day, in a timid way, about politics; when he was through Mansana would exchange a few words with the daughter. She was the living image of her father. He had been corpulent; his face still preserved a certain wrinkled plumpness. She would become just like him, for her little dumpy figure gave promise of this; it possessed, however, that budding fullness to which a morning dress is so becoming, and Mansana never saw her in anything else. The father's eyes were feeble and watery; hers were half closed, her head, too, she kept slightly bowed. The little individual's face and figure had great powers of attraction in this quiet intercourse. Her hair was carefully done up, day after day, in the latest style; this betrayed a desire on the part of the child of the cloister to be one with this wicked world. Those small plump hands that were so well poised on the firmly-knit wrists, were always busied with some dainty bit of needle-work which the head was bowed over and the half-closed eyes followed. She raised the drooping lids when Mansana addressed her, but usually bestowed only a side glance on him, although she did not wholly look away. The yet undeveloped soul of a child peeped forth from her eyes half shyly, half joyously, but with thorough curiosity, on the new world she had entered, and on this new person she had found in it. The more one gazes into such half-closed eyes, the more they fascinate, inasmuch as they never wholly reveal their hidden depths. So far as hers were concerned, there was often something roguish lurking in their corners, and what they actually thought of *him* — aye, that Mansana would have given much to know. And simply in order to gain favor in her eyes he told her more about himself than he had ever in his life told to any one person. It diverted him to watch her two dimples coming and going while he talked, and the continual play about the small mouth, which was as red and as sweet as an untouched berry.

But it diverted him still more when, with a voice whose innocent tones rang in his mind like the warbling of birds on a parched summer morning, she began bashfully but inquisitively to question him about his approaching marriage. Her ideas concerning betrothals and wedding-trips, if not directly expressed, at least peeping out all over her questions, were so enchanting that they restored the old charm to the subject itself.

To *her* it was due that ten or twelve days

after his arrival in this place Theresa actually received a letter from him, and immediately afterward several others.

He was no master of the pen; his letters, therefore, were as brief as his conversations; that they became ardent was due again to the little one. Every morning after breakfast he wrote; the fact was, he took so lively a pleasure in those innocent morning conversations, surveying the fresh girlish form, the deft fingers that were engaged in the needle-work, the harmony of mouth, eyes, and dimples, enjoying the tones of her voice, that all his old yearnings were revived.

Quite a contrast to the little one did Theresa present in all her superb grandeur of body and mind, when he sat at his desk holding converse with her. Even now he could not smile at her vehemence, yet how magnanimous was her acceptance of his silence: —

"It did not worry me in the least. *Of course you should not have written!* You needed rest even from me; you ought to have been free from my letters, too, at all events from their impetuosity. But forgive me! This is *your* fault alone, as *I* alone am to blame for what you now suffer. I can never forgive myself, but will endeavor to make amends to you through all the rest of my life!"

Not one in a thousand would have thought and written thus; he was forced to admit this to himself — and at the same time that she always exhausted him. In order to become more composed and calm, he wrote her about Amanda Brandini, — that was the young girl's name.

He repeated a conversation the little one had had with him about weddings and marriages. It seemed to him very attractive, and he thought he had expressed it so well that he could not help reading the letter over a second time.

The sprightly morning meetings, over which he rejoiced the whole day long, were never followed by an invitation to visit father and daughter in their own home. This honorable reserve pleased Mansana and the interviews awakened ever greater and greater longings for Theresa. How unspeakably was not the princess surprised when she received a telegram announcing that he would meet her in Ancona in three days, — he yearned for her.

The day the telegram was sent he happened to be lounging about a square, on which was a café, and feeling thirsty he entered it. He sat looking out on the square, while waiting to be served, — he had never been there before. Suddenly he discovered Amanda Brandini or a balcony opposite. So that was where she lived.

But at her side and leaning over the railing, as she was doing, and so near her that he could breathe her breath, stood a gay young lieutenant. He had been presented that same forenoon to Mansana, who had heard that he was from a neighboring garrison, and that he was usually called "the Amorin."

But now "the Amorin's" eyes hung on hers; they were both smiling, while their lips moved, and as what they were saying could not be heard it looked to Mansana as though they were whispering confidentially together. They never seemed to get through.

Giuseppe Mansana felt the blood rush to his heart, and he experienced a burning pain. He rose and strode away, then remembered that he had not paid for what he had left behind untouched, turned and settled his account. When he got outside and again looked up, he was surprised to see the two in the balcony engaged in wrestling. "The Amorin" was urging something, she was defending herself, as red as blood. The struggle set off her figure, her eagerness, her face. "The Amorin's" insolent assurance called forth a tumultuous opposition. Who had admitted such a house-breaker? Where was her father?

CHAPTER X.

The next morning Mansana sat earlier than was his wont on the bench; but the other two also came earlier. They, too, must find satisfaction in the interviews and desire to prolong them, now that but two yet remained. From the inevitable political introduction with the father, he suddenly turned toward Amanda with, —

"Who was that you were wrestling with on the balcony yesterday?"

Her face became suffused with the loveliest blushes, while her eyelids drooped even more than usual; still she tried to look at him.

A young girl blushes, indeed, at everything, but this Mansana did not know. He grew quite as pale as she was rosy. This alarmed her; he saw it, and misinterpreted this also.

The father, who had been listening with open mouth, broke out, —

"Ah, now I understand! Luigi, my sister's son, Luigi Borghi! Yes, he is in town on a visit of a few days; will remain for the town festival. Ha, ha, he is a madcap!"

But Giuseppe Mansana went straight from this interview to his friend Major Sardi, the man for whose sake he had chosen this especial garrison, and asked him about Luigi's character. It was bad.

Thence he went to the young man himself, who lived at a hotel and had just risen. Luigi Borghi greeted his superior officer respectfully and with many apologies. They both took seats.

"I leave here to-morrow to be married," began Mansana. "I mention this in order that what I am about to say may be understood — as it is meant. I have, during my brief sojourn here, taken a great liking to an innocent young girl. Her name is Brandini."

"Ah, Amanda!"

"She is your cousin?"

"Yes, she is."

"Do you stand in any other relation to her? Do you intend to marry her?"

"No — but" —

"I have no other motive in questioning you about this than that of a gentleman. You need not reply, if you object."

"Certainly not! I repeat it with pleasure: I do not intend to marry Amanda; she is very poor."

"Very well. Why, then, do you go as you do to the house? Why do you call forth sentiments in her to which you have no thought of responding, and which may so easily be misinterpreted?"

"Your last remark seems to me to imply an accusation."

"To be sure. You are known to be a reckless libertine."

"Signore!" and the young lieutenant rose to his feet.

At once the tall captain did the same.

"I, Giuseppe Mansana, say this, and am at your service."

But little Luigi Borghi had no fancy to be slain at such an early and interesting age by the first fencer in the army. And so he was silent, and his eyes sought the ground.

"Either you will promise me never to enter her house again, never to seek her society, or you will have to answer for your conduct to me. I have resolved to settle this before I leave. Why do you hesitate?"

"Because, as an officer, I cannot be known to have been compelled "—

"To do a good deed? You may thank your God if you can be! Perhaps I have presented the subject in the wrong way. I should undoubtedly have said to you: 'Do what I ask of you, and you shall be my friend, and may count on me in whatever straits you may come!'"

"I would gladly have for my friend so great an officer, and would be proud to be able to count on Giuseppe Mansana's generous aid."

"Very well. Then you promise what I ask?"

"I promise!"

"Thank you! Your hand!"

"With all my heart!"

"Farewell!"

"Farewell!"

Two hours later Mansana went down to the toledo of the little town. There, outside of a shop, stood Amanda and Luigi, engaged in a conversation which seemed to be highly entertaining to both, for they were laughing heartily. The father was inside of the shop, paying for some purchases. None of them saw Mansana until he was in their midst. His pale, sallow face sufficed to send Amanda flying in terror to her father; but the still more appalled lieutenant remained where he was and said, retreating a step, —

"I assure you, signore, I was requested to come here! And we — we were not laughing at you."

At that moment a shriek from Amanda rang

out of the shop. It was caused by Giuseppe Mansana's appearance, as he, without a word, without a gesture, made a stride forward, just one, toward her little cousin. There was a leopard's seven-ells leap in this stride; the next moment Luigi might be a dead man.

But every one in the shop and on the street turned to the young girl who had uttered the shriek, and who stood nestled up to her father. From her the eyes of the by-standers wandered in all directions. There was nothing to be seen. Two officers stood quietly outside in the street conversing together. What was the matter? Those who were outside came into the shop, and all gathered about Amanda. What was it? But she, exposed, for the first time in her life, to the gaze and questions of the multitude, stood aghast, and her father, who had failed to obtain an answer, became bewildered. Then Mansana parted asunder the group about her, and with a silent air of command offered her his arm; she hastened to accept it and walked away with him; her father followed.

When they were out of ear-shot, Mansana said, —

"It is my duty to tell you that your kinsman, Lieutenant Borghi, is a profligate wretch, who deserves and shall receive chastisement."

How alarmed Amanda was again: first to hear that Luigi was a profligate wretch, although she did not exactly know what that meant, and next that Luigi was to receive chastisement, although she knew not why. She gazed this time with wide-open eyes into Mansana's face; but looked none the wiser. Her lips, too, parted. A great curiosity began to break through her fear; Mansana detected it, — and angry as he had just been he now could not but smile at such intensely stupid innocence, and its ludicrous and bewitching expression. And thus suddenly thrown into a good-humor again, he even observed at last what a comical appearance the father presented. The old gentleman was like a school-boy who has been listening to ghost stories in the dark. In order to show Mansana how thoroughly he understood all that was horrible, he manifested a profound gratitude and begged him to accompany them home.

This Mansana did; and Amanda, who hoped she might learn something more, clung to him in the most deferential and insinuating manner. He began by conjecturing her purpose, and it amused him; but ended by forgetting this and feeling jubilant delight over the melodious murmur of her voice, over each roguish word, and at the thought that her sweet lips, about which the dimples came and went, her half-closed eyes, in their enigmatical play, and her harmonious nature, for one moment were wholly consecrated to him, and that this fresh, youthful form, in all the fullness of its beauty, lived and breathed in his proximity.

The next morning their last interview was to take place; but no, it was not permitted to be the last; he must come to them the next afternoon, for he was not to leave until evening. He went from them in an ecstasy of delight.

The soothing influence she exercised over him, manifested itself also by impelling him to present himself that same afternoon in the unfortunate Luigi's room and asking his pardon. *He* was not to blame for meeting his cousin in the street and being accosted by her.

"And if you were laughing at me" —

"But we were not, indeed!" protested the frightened "Amorin."

"You surely had a right. My zeal was rather absurd. I am aware of it now. Here is my hand!"

This was hastily seized, a few disconnected words were spoken, and Mansana left — in undisputed supremacy, as he had come.

The little lieutenant, who had been feeling

like one who had death for his companion, was seized with a dizzy joy. He sprang up in the air and burst into the loudest peals of laughter. Mansana heard this laughter, and paused on the stairs. Luigi shuddered at his imprudence, and when there came once more a knock at the door he was too terrified to say, " Come in ! " But the door was opened, nevertheless.

"Was that you who were laughing?" inquired Mansana.

"No, on my honor!" replied the "Amorin," gesticulating with both hands. Mansana stood for a while contemplating him.

But when he was gone again, the exultation returned. Luigi could not help it. And as he dared neither scream nor dance, he *must* communicate it to some one. This he did at the officers' café among his former classmates. It created great merriment. Over the wine-cup witticisms fell like hail upon the unlucky captain, who on the eve of his wedding with a princess created a scandal by falling in love with a little boarding-school miss.

Major Sardi, Mansana's friend, was witness to this.

The next morning Mansana had his last interview on the heights. It began much earlier than usual, and ended much later, and not until the door of father and daughter's house was reached. In the afternoon he was to call according to promise to take leave. Half roguishly, half languishingly, exactly as she felt about it, Amanda discussed the wedding, for to a well brought-up Italian girl marriage is the portal that leads to all earthly bliss, that is to the state in which uncertainty, restraint, and annoyances cease, and in which perpetual peace, new dresses, carriage drives, and evenings at the opera begin! Her sweet babble was but the song of his own longings; her dainty little person invested this song with increased fullness, so that the realization of his approaching happiness impelled him to tell the young girl of the part she had had in it. Little Amanda shed tears at this, — a young girl's tears are so ready to flow when anything kind is said about her. And then she could not help telling him how much confidence she felt in him. She mentioned this because she had always been a trifle uneasy in his presence; but she did not say so. Since, therefore, it was not as true as she would herself have wished, she added a smile. This was to strengthen her words. But where the smile shone the atmosphere was still full of tears, and it formed there (I mean within Mansana's own breast) an inconceivably beautiful rainbow. He took her round little hand in both of his: that was his farewell. He said something, moreover, but knew not what himself; she grew rosy red. He saw her brow, arms, and head above him on the stairs, and again from the balcony. He heard floating out over the square a melodious "Farewell!" and still another — and then he turned into a side street.

He had not noticed the approach of Sardi, had not seen that the latter was making directly for him, and he was roused in bewilderment by a slap on the shoulder.

"Is it really true?" laughed Sardi. "Are you in love with the little one up yonder? — you actually look so!"

Mansana's face became copper-colored, his eyes had a fixed stare, his breath came and went hastily.

"What is that you say?" asked he. "How do you know" — He paused. He certainly would not himself tell what he first wanted to hear, whether any one could have — whether Luigi had — "What is that you say?" he repeated.

"Upon my soul! You are not getting embarrassed; are you?"

"What is that you say?" reiterated Mansana, redder than before, knitting his brow, and laying one hand, not very gently, on the major's shoulder.

This offended Sardi. Mansana's violence, indeed, came upon him so unexpectedly that he had no time for reflection ; but in self-defense, and in order to annoy the friend who had given way to so unjust an outburst of wrath, he repeated to Mansana what people already said, and how he had been made sport of at the officers' café.

Mansana's wrath knew no bounds. He swore that if Sardi did not forthwith state who had dared such a thing, he himself must give satisfaction for it. The two friends were actually on the verge of a challenge. But Sardi finally so far regained his self-possession that he was able to represent to the other what an unpleasant noise it would create if Mansana should fight with him or any one else about his correct relations with Amanda Brandini, and that, too, on the eve of his departure for his wedding with Princess Leaney. The best answer would certainly be to leave and celebrate his nuptials. Hereupon a fresh ebullition of wrath from Mansana. He was able to attend to his own affairs and defend his own honor. Out with the names! Sardi could find no reason for concealing these, and gave them one by one, adding that if it would gratify him to kill all these young lads, he might if he chose! Mansana wanted to go forthwith to the officers' café, as though they were all still there. Sardi succeeded in convincing him of the folly of this; then he insisted upon at least seeking Borghi without delay. Now Sardi expressed a willingness to present a challenge to Borghi; "but," said he, "on what grounds should he be challenged."

"For what he has said!" shrieked the other.

"Why, what has he said? That you are in love with Amanda Brandini? And are you not?"

Had Mansana set forth without meeting Sardi, he would have been married a few days later to Princess Leaney. Now, on the contrary, this was what took place: —

Mansana: "Do you presume to say that I love Amanda?"

Sardi: "I merely ask. But if you do *not* love her, how the deuce does it concern you if the whelp does say so, or if he loves her himself — or leads her astray?"

"You are a brutal scoundrel to speak so!"

"Pray, what are *you* who attack a young relative merely because he jokes with her" —

" Jokes with her!"

Mansana clinched his fists and pressed his lips together.

" Who will look after them when you are gone?" Sardi hastened to remark.

" I am not going away!" shrieked Mansana.

" Not going away! Have you lost your senses?"

" I am not going away!" repeated Mansana, with hands and arms uplifted, as though he were taking a solemn oath.

Sardi was alarmed.

" Then you do love her, after all," he whispered.

Mansana gave way completely! Deep groans were heard; his powerful frame was shaken by them. Sardi feared a stroke of apoplexy. Finally Mansana seemed, as it were, to rise superior to himself, his countenance shone, and slowly, perfectly self-possessed, he said, —

"I love her!" and then turning to Sardi: " I shall not leave!"

And from this moment he was like a tempest: he turned, looked above and beyond him, and stormily sped onward.

" Where are you going?" asked Sardi, hastenng after him.

" To Borghi."

"But I thought I was to go to him!"

"Then go!"

"But where are *you* going?"

"To Borghi!" And pausing, he added, in an ecstasy, —

"I love her. Any one who wants to take her from me *shall die!*"

He was about to proceed on his way.

"But does *she* love you?" shrieked Sardi, forgetting that they stood in the street.

Mansana stretched forth his sinewy hands and said in a hollow voice, —

"*She shall love me.*"

Sardi was frightened.

"Giuseppe, you are mad!" said he. "The high pitch to which you have been worked up was more than you could bear. Now it has only assumed new force and centred in a new object. You are not yourself! — Giuseppe — do not run away from me! Can you not see that the people on the street are noticing you?"

Then Mansana stood still.

"Do you know why I became ill, Cornelio? Because I paid attention to the people on the street? I was *forced* to keep silent, to hear, to be trampled on! That was what made me ill." He advanced a step nearer to Sardi.

"Now I will shriek it aloud to the whole world: I love her!"

He actually did shriek aloud, then turned and walked on with a proud bearing. Sardi followed and took him by the arm. He guided him into a still narrower street, but Mansana seemed wholly unconscious of it. He merely walked on, talking in a loud voice, and gesticulating.

"What would it be for me to become Princess Leaney's husband," said he, "and to be the manager of her ladyship's property and the servant of her ladyship's caprices?"

And here he gave loose reins to his deeply wounded self-love.

"Now for the first time I admit to myself the whole truth: it would have been an unworthy life for Giuseppe Mansana."

Sardi thought that if the reticent and at least outwardly modest Giuseppe Mansana could suddenly begin thus to shout and boast, any other inconceivable thing might occur; and with a perseverance and ingenuity that did him honor he endeavored to persuade his friend to take a short trip, if only for a couple of days, in order to gain light on the emotions and circumstances that were submerging him. But he might as well have talked at a hurricane.

CHAPTER XI.

THAT same evening Amanda, in the greatest secrecy, received a letter, which made her exceedingly curious. She struck a light and read it. It was from Luigi! — the first she had ever received from him. It read thus: —

AMANDA, — A madman is in pursuit of me and wants to kill me. An hour ago I was obliged to give him a solemn promise — indeed, I have signed my name to it — to relinquish all claims on you forever, and not even to speak to you! This was cowardice, I well know. I despise myself, as you must despise me.

But the way this came about was that not until I had given my word did I know that I loved you. Perhaps I did not do so before. But now I love you beyond all bounds, and never in the world has there been a more unhappy mortal than I am.

I cannot conceive of the possibility of its being all over! It cannot be so forever. It depends, though, altogether on yourself, Amanda, if you do not despise me too greatly. For if you love me the madman will accomplish nothing, and so some day things must change again.

I am like a man in prison. I cannot stir. But this I know, that if you do not help me out again, I shall die.

Amanda! A word, a sign! It is too dangerous to write. I know not how I shall manage to get this to you. Do not *you* try to send a letter to me. He may be on the scent. But to-morrow at the festival! Be there, near the band, stay there until I have found you. Then speak only with your eyes! If they are friendly, I shall know all. Ah, Amanda, the rest will come of itself when once you are mine! Amanda,

Your devoted and unhappy cousin,
LUIGI.

The moment Amanda had read this letter she knew that she loved Luigi. Never before had she looked into this matter. But now she loved him beyond measure, of this she was sure.

There must be some misunderstanding about what Mansana had said concerning him, and the promise Luigi had made of course did not amount to anything. Girls do not accept such things very literally when they seem improbable to them. Moreover, Mansana had now gone away.

And so, the next day, the festival day, a

lovely autumn day, she was astir betimes in the morning; the band had passed at sunrise and the cannons had sent forth their thundering peals. The church, decorated within and without, was crowded, and little Amanda might be seen at her father's side, among the worshipers, dressed in her choicest finery. She prayed for Luigi. When she had finished she practiced smiling. She was resolved to offer Luigi consolation through the most friendly look she could command. When the procession was over and noon had passed, she hastened to the appointed spot; the band was already playing on the market-place. She so urged her old father on that they were among the first grown people who arrived, but for that reason among those who were most wedged in before an hour had elapsed. She looked at her father's perspiring face and thought of her own and what a horrid appearance it would present to Luigi. She must get out of the crowd, let it cost what it might; and yet the price should not be a rose or a knot of ribbon, or even the least exertion, for that would cause her to grow redder than she now was. She therefore made but little progress.

Yet, alas! she grew hotter and hotter. She heard the big drum and a couple of bass horns, through the thunder of thousands of voices and laughter in which she was submerged; she saw the tower on the municipal building, and the clapper which extended below the bell, and which was the last object she beheld above the human billows that closed about her. Her father's pitiable face told her how red and odious she must appear — and the little one began to weep.

But Luigi, too, had been among the first to reach the band; and as neither the town nor the square in front of the municipal building were large, the two who were seeking each other amid the thronging multitude could not well avoid at last standing face to face. He saw her, rosy with blushes, smiling through her tears. He took her blushes for those of joy, her tears for those of sympathy, and her smile for what it was intended. The father, in his anxiety and distress, hailed Luigi as an angel of deliverance and cried, —

"Help us, Luigi."

And Luigi promptly set to work to do as he was bid. The task was no easy one; indeed both Amanda and her father were several times in actual danger, and Luigi felt himself a hero. With elbows and back he defended them, and never once removing his eyes from Amanda, he drank deeply from her long, timid gaze. He did not speak; he did not break his oath! This, too, gave him a proud consciousness; there must be an air of nobility about him, and he felt from the reflection in Amanda's eyes that he really did appear noble.

But no earthly happiness is of long duration. Giuseppe Mansana had about a quarter of an hour previous to this descried Luigi in the crowd, and with the instinct that jealousy possesses, had watched him from afar, an easy matter for one of Mansana's height. Luigi, in his restless search, had constantly worked his way forward, and had thus no idea of the danger close at hand; and now he was so engrossed with his task of deliverance, or, in other words, in reflecting his noble image in Amanda's eyes, that he perceived nothing until Mansana's hyena face was directly opposite his, and he felt his scorching breath on his cheeks.

Amanda gave one of her well-known screams, her father became frightfully stupid, and Luigi disappeared.

At the same moment, Amanda had drawn one arm through Mansana's and placed the warm, gloved hand of the other on his; two bewitching, half-closed eyes, brimming over with roguishness, fear, and entreaty, looked up into his face. They were just out of the throng, it was possible to understand what was said, and Mansana heard from a voice, which might ring the angels into heaven, —

"Papa and I have been in great danger. It was so nice that we got help!" and he felt the pressure of her hand.

Now Mansana had seen those same eyes dwelling on Luigi's face, and there rushed through his mind a thought which later in life he took up again a thousand times but now lost the moment it came, and this thought was, "I am certainly entangled in a stupid, meaningless affair."

The little prattler by his side continued, —

"Poor Luigi met us just at our extremity. Papa begged him to help us, and he did so without speaking a word. We did not even get to thank him." And directly after: "It is really delightful that you have not left yet. Now you must go home with us that we may have a good talk! We had such a nice one the last time."

And her full, young bosom fluttered beneath its silken covering, her round wrist quivered above her glove, the tips of her little feet moved restlessly below her dress; her rosy lips bubbled over with chatter and laughter, and those two eyes of hers beamed in half-concealed familiarity, — and Mansana was borne along with them.

He did not mention Luigi's name; it remained like a dagger-point in his heart; it entered the deeper the more charming she became. This struggle between pain and love made him absolutely silent. But all the busier were her sweet lips, while she gave him a seat and brought forward fruits, which she herself peeled and handed to him. She went into a little ecstasy of delight that their meetings on the heights were not yet interrupted; indeed, she proposed a little excursion farther up the slope, which they must make the next morning; she would bring breakfast along. Still he had only succeeded in uttering a few monosyllables. He could not break in upon this innocent idyl with his passion; and yet the struggle within was so terrible that he could bear it no longer, and was compelled to leave.

No sooner was he down the steps and the last greeting had been sent from the balcony, than the little charmer, who had been so unwearied in her flattering attentions, closed tightly the balcony door and flung herself sobbing on her knees before her father. He was not in the east surprised. He had the same fear as she;

Mansana's last look as he left, as well as his whole presence, had filled the room with such a fateful atmosphere, that if in the next moment they had all exploded it would not in the least have surprised him. And when, through her tears, she whispered, " Father, we must leave here ! " he merely replied, " Yes, my child, of course we must ! "

It was essential to depart secretly, and therefore, if possible, that very night.

CHAPTER XII.

GIUSEPPE MANSANA had been at Borghi's room and had not found him ; at the officers' café and not found him ; later, about amongst the festal throng, but had met him nowhere. On the other hand, he had encountered many officers, and civilians, too, in company with them, who seemed to him to relapse into silence when they saw him, and to talk in low tones together as he passed them.

Whatever manner of game it might be that he was engaged in, lose he must not. His honor forbade it.

Exhausted in body and soul, he sat late in the evening on the watch in front of the café, facing the Brandini apartment. There was a light in Amanda's window. She was packing up the few articles she and her father were to take with them, for in order to give their departure the appearance of a short trip they were to leave most of their things behind.

But Mansana thought: this light is perhaps a signal. And sure enough, when Amanda was weary from excitement and work, she went out on the balcony to take a few breaths of fresh air; she could be seen so plainly by the light behind her; she looked down along the street. Was she expecting any one from that direction? Yes, indeed, steps were heard there They came nearer. A man appeared. He went in the line of the house toward Amanda's balcony; now he walked past a lantern; Mansana saw an officer's cap and a beardless face; he saw Amanda bow lower toward the street. A young girl who loves, actually thinks she sees the beloved object in every place, at all times and especially one whom she loves in fear The officer walked more slowly when he descried her; under the balcony he paused and looked up. Amanda hastened into the house and closed the door; the officer walked on.

Had they agreed on a trysting-place? Mansana started full run across the square; but the officer had already turned the corner, and when Mansana reached it the officer was no longer in the street. Into which house had he disappeared? It would not do to rouse the whole street to find out; he must give up the search.

By so trifling an incident as that of a young officer, who dwelt in the neighborhood, passing beneath a balcony on which a young damsel was standing alone, — by so trifling an occurrence as this, Mansana's destiny was fulfilled.

He went to bed that night, not to sleep, but to vow to himself over and over again, in the anguish of his heart, that the next morning she should be his, or he would not live.

But the next morning she was not on the heights. He waited an hour and still no one came. Then he went to her house. Before the door to the lodgings of the Brandinis stood an old woman, with their breakfast and a note. As Mansana was about to seize the knocker, the old woman said, "There is no one at home here, as it seems. But read this note that was hanging on the knocker." Mansana took it. "Gone away. More later. B." He let the note fall and strode away. The old woman called after him to ask what was in the note. But he made no reply.

Princess Leaney, on reaching Ancona the next day and not meeting Mansana on the platform, experienced great anxiety; she knew not why. She went herself to the telegraph office and sent him hearty greetings, which plainly expressed her fear. She then hastened home and waited; her alarm grew with every hour. Finally the telegram was returned with the money that had been paid for the reply message. Captain Mansana had left the town.

Terror overpowered her. The self-reproaches in which she had daily lived became mountains; they shut out every prospect. She must go where he was, find him, talk with him, tend him; she suspected the worst. Evening found her at the railway station, accompanied by a single servant.

In the dawn of the morning the next day she was walking back and forth at the junction with the road from the west. There were not many travelers at the station, and those who were there she did not see. All the more did they look at her as she swept past them, back and forth, wrapped in a white fur cloak which she had so thrown over her shoulders that the arms hung loose, and with a fur cap on her head, beneath which her floating hair and veil had become entangled. The large eyes and the whole face evinced emotion and weariness. In her restless walk she often passed by a tall lady, plainly clad, who stood gazing intently at the luggage-van, where several men were busied. Another time when the princess passed, there appeared an officer who addressed the lady, and to a question from the luggage-van answered, —

" Mansana."

The princess rushed toward him.

" Mansana ? " cried she.

" Princess Leaney ? " whispered the officer in astonishment, as he bowed to her.

" Major Sardi ! " she said, in reply, adding, hastily : " Mansana ! Did you mention Mansana ? "

" Yes, this is his mother."

As he introduced them, the mother drew her veil aside, and there was such power in her face to arouse the confidence of the princess that the latter threw herself into her arms as into a sure refuge from all sorrowing thoughts, and then she burst into passionate tears. Mansana's mother silently embraced her, but stood as one who was waiting. She patted her affectionately but said nothing.

When Theresa could command words she asked, —

"Where is he?"

"None of us know," replied the mother, calmly.

"But we hope to know soon," added Sardi.

The princess sprang up, white as chalk, staring at them both.

"What has happened?" cried she.

The thoughtful mother, who had braved so many storms, said quietly, —

"We have doubtless the same journey before us. Let us take a compartment to ourselves, and then we can talk matters over and hold counsel together."

This was done.

CHAPTER XIII.

THE Brandini family had gone to the home of Nina Borghi, Brandini's sister and Luigi's mother. It so chanced that on the same night train by which the Brandinis fled, the hero

Luigi also took flight. They discovered one another at a station late the next morning, as Luigi was about to leave the train. He was so alarmed that he would have pushed past them without speaking; but old Brandini held fast to him and poured into his ear his tale of woe. Luigi merely said, —

"Go to mother," and hastened away.

He went, however, to the telegraph office immediately on reaching his garrison, and, in a very excited frame of mind, telegraphed to his mother announcing her brother's approach. The telegram was couched in such anxious words that the lady to whom it was addressed, and who lived alone outside of Castellamare, near Naples, became much alarmed. She was not less so when her brother and his daughter arrived and told her what threatened both them and her son.

Captain Mansana had conjectured that the Brandinis had gone south, for there was no night train on any but the southern route. He followed. But after vainly seeking during two days a starting-point for further investigations, he turned about and directed his course toward the town where Luigi Borghi was stationed. *He* must know where the two were, and this knowledge he should impart to him or take the consequences! As Mansana was aware that he was well known in the town, he went to work with great caution, in order that Luigi might have no warning. Consequently he was obliged to pass two days in the town before he met him. This occurred on the street, when Mansana had been searching for him in one of the little cafés of the townspeople. To his astonishment, Luigi was not frightened, as he had expected to find him. And to his still greater astonishment, Luigi unhesitatingly told where the Brandini family were. Mansana became suspicious. He called Luigi's attention to what it would cost to speak anything but the truth, but the little officer did not even blink as he swore that what he said was true.

Further settlement with the lieutenant must be postponed. That same day Mansana took the train south.

What did he want? Uncompromisingly the same: she should be his! This was why Luigi had been so leniently treated. Since Amanda's warily undertaken flight, there was a tempest raging within Mansana's soul; no one should venture to treat him thus unpunished. He did not love her; no, he hated her, and that was why she should be his! If not!— This brief train of thought kept revolving round and round in his mind. The air was filled with confused pictures of his comrades standing in groups laughing at him. He certainly had been made a fool of by a little girl just out of a convent, and a little lieutenant just out of school!

How it had come so far that this conflict with two insignificant children should be the end of his proud career, he could not make clear to himself.

Princess Leaney's image — which during his first excitement rarely rose up before him and was angrily thrust aside when it did appear — kept growing clearer and clearer the more exhausted and ashamed he became. She was the goal of the life for which he was destined, so lofty was his aim! And he thought no longer of her rank, but of the glowing course of her thoughts, of the beauty of her presence, exalted by the admiration of all mortals.

Amanda's image sank away at the same time. He was not sure but that she was round-shouldered. He was actually able to speculate upon this.

People who have made us ridiculous in our own eyes and those of others are not very apt to be the gainers thereby. And when Mansana had reached the point where he could discover that Amanda's figure was awkward, her face and conversation insignificant, her voice drawling, her hair absurdly arranged, her flattery much too soft and insinuating, he asked himself if it would not be the most ludicrous thing in the world to compel such a person to become Signora Mansana. No, there was something that would be still more absurd, and that was to kill himself for her sake.

What should he do, then? Go back to the princess? That path was barred — barred by his pride a hundred thousand times! *Past* Amanda and onward, to the Spanish civil war, for instance? An adventurer's career, hollow, empty! Just as well end his life at home.

Turn back and let all be as before? The princess lost, the admiration of his comrades lost, faith in himself lost! The only way in which he could return was at her side, that cursed little woman! With her by the hand he could appear as victor, and if he must pay for this prize with an unhappy life, so it must be. His honor would then be saved, and no one should be allowed to read his soul.

There would be actual glory in having rejected a wealthy princess, and captured the daughter of a poor pensioned officer, in a conflict even with herself! But the moment he reached this conclusion, his soul revolted at all the deception which such an honor as this must contain. He sprang up from his seat in the compartment, but sat down again; — there were several passengers within.

The train proceeded onward toward his goal. What a goal! Ruin was inevitable, his life must surely be sacrificed to honor; and this whether honor was attained or no.

The merciful power of sleep intervened. He dreamed of his mother. Her large, noble eyes hung over him like a heaven. He wept and was awakened. There was an old man in the compartment who was deeply affected by his tears. Just then the train stopped. They were in the vicinity of Naples; Mansana got out. The morning was glorious. The clear sky, bordered by the faint outlines of the chain of hills, served as a reminder and a warning; he shivered in the chill morning air and returned to the smoke of the locomotive which was just starting, to the rumbling and din of the train as it stormed onward, and to his own stinging thoughts.

Farther on, as they passed along the seashore, he would have given much if the train had deviated from its course and slowly and smoothly glided out into the trackless waters What gentle deliverance in such a death!

He hid himself in his corner when the train stopped at Naples; in the vast human throng about the station there might be some one who knew him. The day became more and more glorious while the train glided through the coast towns along the sea; the sun was mild as on a summer morning, and its rays in the hazy sea atmosphere cast a tinge over mountain, sea, and the entire landscape. When he got out of the compartment and was driving toward his destination, and still more after he had dismissed the carriage and was climbing the steep cliffs, with the sea at his feet and the grand view over the gulf, bordered with islands that looked like shapeless sea-monsters on guard, and with mountains under the dominion of Vesuvius and towns gleaming white beneath a slow smoke, then he felt a sense of life — not his *own life* which was but a chase after honor, a struggle, he knew not himself for what, *now* that this struggle had ended in absolutely nothing — no, life as it was meant to be beneath God's high arching heavens, in the splendor of *His* glory which overspread all nature and thus extended beyond the goal which life usually marks out.

He approached the last hill, on which the house he was seeking was situated. Soon he saw the house, which stood beyond the summit of the hill, surrounded by a high, sharp-pointed iron fence. Then his heart began to throb. There could be no mistake; he had, moreover, taken the route accurately pointed out by the coachman.

So this was the place! And before his feelings were clear to his own mind, she appeared on the balcony, she, Amanda, in her bright morning gown, with a smile on her lips, as if she had said or heard something amusing as she stepped out. She saw him at once, uttered her well-known scream and ran in.

As a weary huntsman when suddenly brought face to face with his game regains all his elasticity, so Mansana felt rising within him a wild power, an untamed purpose, and before he knew what he was about, he stood at the gate of the iron fence and had bounded over it without ringing the bell. Controlled by his own lively emotions, all his warrior-like instincts were aroused; he turned at once and possessed himself of the key which was on the inner side of the gate. The door to the house was half closed; he pushed it open. He was admitted to a large, bright vestibule. Colored glass cast its own peculiar play over some small statues, a mosaic inlaid stone floor and vases, filled with palms, fan-palms, and flowers. On a pair of antique sofas were lying, on one a straw hat with blue ribbons — was it hers? — on the other a parasol of a peculiar watered material with a costly carved handle whose end was studded with a large blue stone. He recognized it, and a wounded feeling followed the recollections evoked, but he made no effort to explain this. For now he rang the bell. He must make haste.

No one came to open the door. He began to shiver, then tried to control himself, but failed. He could not remain longer thus. If he could not execute his purpose at once he was lost. He rang once more. His will rose with the act. Now it was necessary to make or break. The door to the room opened, a bright light flooded the vestibule; the stained glass did not permit him to see more than that the person who was approaching and who closed the door behind her was blue and tall. As soon as the door was closed all became dark in the hall. Who could it be? Might not the house chance to be filled with people? An actual terror seized him at this thought, which had not occurred to him a moment before. What mad pranks, what complications, what interferences, and inconvenient persons might not here assail him! He was perhaps entering a bee-hive of provoked anger and resistance; it might prove to be a fool's errand he was on! *No, on such an errand he would not go a second time!* And he put on the whole armor of his will, and made sure that his weapon was by him. Then the large door was thrown wide open, and before him in the lofty doorway —

Yes, there in the lofty doorway stood Theresa Leaney, clad in blue, and very pale.

And he? He stood there motionless, his self-possession gone.

The door was wide open; they stood on either side of the threshold. Silent as themselves was all within and without. At last she extended her right hand. There ran a tremor through his frame; she stretched out both arms; he rushed into her ready embrace with a ring like that of an instrument which has been struck. And he took her up in his arms, bore her out to the sofa, sat down with her on his lap, plunged his head against her bosom, and clasping her in a warm embrace, rose up with her in his arms, sat down again and broke into the most vehement flood of tears on her bosom. Not a word of explanation!

He finally put her down beside him on the sofa and flung himself on his knees. He gazed with boundless admiration into her smiling face. Now he was overcome, conquered; never in the world would it have been well with Giuseppe Mansana had it not been so.

And when, in burning gratitude, he raised his eyes, purified by this feeling of humility, it was not hers they met; they fell on another behind him — there stood his mother.

Both he and Theresa arose. Instinctively he sought his mother's hands. When he held them in his own he kissed them, and once more falling on his knees guided them to his head. What had he not experienced since he had so defiantly met her gaze beside his father's bier.

Mansana never got beyond the entrance of this house. The two ladies went back to say farewell; he preceded them down the hill. Why precede them? Because he wanted to put a key quietly in the gate, and because he wished, in all haste and shame, to fling a revolver into the sea. These things accomplished, he sank down on a stone, overwhelmed with fear, joy, gratitude, dismay, — all inextricably blended. The two who followed him, accompanied by a servant with their luggage, saw him sitting below the road, with his head in his hands. They walked together to the railway station.

He did not need to hear much in order to understand how this meeting had come about. It was Sardi who had summoned them; they had sought Luigi Borghi in hopes that *he* would be informed about the Brandinis, and that Mansana would sooner or later find his way to them. That was why Luigi had been so courageously frank, because he knew the two ladies to be already at his mother's house.

Mansana had relapsed into silence.

The wise mother had a foreboding of danger, and begged for rest at Naples, declaring that she needed it herself. They went to a quiet suburban hotel. Here, after much resistance, Mansana's mother got him to bed. And when at last he slept, it seemed as though he would never again awaken. Almost the whole of the next day passed. When he did awake he found himself alone; he was confused and became alarmed, but a few trifles in the room reminded him of his mother and Theresa; he laid back again and slept like a happy child. This time, however, he did not sleep as long as before, for hunger awoke him. He ate, but fell asleep again. For several days and nights he slept, almost without interruption. But when he rose from his couch he was very quiet. He retired more and more into brooding silence.

This was just what his mother had anticipated.

CHAPTER XIV.

The end shall be told by a letter from Theresa Leaney to Mansana's mother. It was dated from the writer's estate in Hungary, not long after the events last related.

Beloved Mother, — At last you shall have a connected account of everything since we parted at Naples. If I repeat anything that I have written before you must pardon me.

Well, then, after our marriage his illness gave place to an eager, humble zeal in serving me, which made me anxious, for it was so unlike him. Upon the whole he was neither confiding nor self-reliant, until after we had been in the town where he was last stationed. He understood perfectly why you wished us to go there first. Ah, how amiable he was there! He began forthwith to run the gauntlet among his comrades, I may say in the most dauntless manner. I can tell you, furthermore, about a young wife who aided him. She had never been happier or more elegant, you see, than when she became the companion of her noble husband in his humiliation; every movement, every expression of her face, every word, seemed, as it were, freighted with "If *I* say nothing, who *then* dare say a word?"

I am, alas, still so much of a coquette that I have a great desire to inform you how I was dressed each of these three days. (I had sent to Ancona for my maid and my wardrobe.) But I will meekly hold my peace.

I am perfectly sure, though, that dearly as a certain young wife was loved after those three days' running the gauntlet in this mountain town, not many women have been loved; for there is power in the temperament you yourself have given from your own soul, you delightful being.

Nor must I forget to sound the praises of the man Sardi. For he *is* a man. He had done such a good thing, in announcing that Mansana was ill, — which he truly was, — and that you and I were his physicians. The good fortune of it all is that he who has won fame among his comrades has also laid up in their hearts treasures on which he may draw for a long time before they are exhausted. People *will* think well of Giuseppe Mansana. He felt this, the dear man, and it made him very humble; for he was sorely oppressed by the thought that he did not deserve it.

In Ancona everything went smoothly; the stubbornness of his nature was conquered. And now he is all mine, — mine the strongest nature in the world, purified and ennobled, — mine the most considerate of masters, the most attentive of servants, — mine the most manly lover that ever Italian girl won. Pardon my strong expressions; I know you do not like them, but they *must* come.

At Bologna — aye, you see I fly — we were walking about and chanced to pass the municipal building. There hang two marble tablets bearing the names of those who fell in the struggle for the town's freedom. Giuseppe's arm trembled, and to this circumstance it was due that we had a conversation than which nothing could form a surer foundation for our union.

You know, beloved mother, how my eyes were opened during the time when I was grieving over the wrong I had done Giuseppe through my despicable caprices, which nearly cost him his life and both of us our happiness. You know that my soul is daily racked with indignation against those public affairs that breed in us defiance, hatred, frenzied fanaticism, culpable intolerance. Unwholesome, unnatural public affairs poison a community and do more harm than the most miserable open warfare; for there is no possibility of estimating how much spiritual strength they consume, how many hearts they bereave, how many homes they lay waste! I assure you, mother, that a land which, for instance, has made an unjust conquest, captured what belongs to others, transforms a whole community into sharers of its guilt, lowers the general moral standard, sharpens the pen of the strategist, the crow-bar of the burglar, the harsh words of the commander — ah! it drives the heart from its rights in the family and in society!

There are some stupid verses that were written about me by an enamored fool; not one word in them is true. But do you know, dearest mother, I feel now that had I not met Giuseppe, those lines might one day have become true, for stupid and heartless as they are I would finally have become equally stupid and heartless! And why so? Because the unhappy state of public affairs had strewed poison into my existence.

And my confessions were brought face to face with Giuseppe's. That defiant, vain will of his had so entirely become his master that the most trifling and chance interference might easily have cost him his life, the most accidental aim have changed his course. But this defiant, vain will, — in what atmosphere was it bred?

We gave each other the most complete confidence, that evening at Bologna. And then for the first time everything seemed so secure; ah, so secure!

Here, on my dearly loved estate he has now set to work. All was chaos here, and he has something now on which he can exercise his will! He wishes to resign; he is determined to be no longer a peace officer. He needs a fixed goal, and one that is close at hand; if I divine rightly it is the one which lies hidden from the world that is dearest to him.

Thus, at all events, matters stand for the present. What later developments may arise I know not. But I do know that if ever Italy be in danger, he will be one of the first — and that in all respects.

God bless you! Come up here soon. You must see him in his busy life, and you must see him with me. Has ever mortal at any time had so considerate a husband, so noble a lover? Ah, I forgot — my extravagant expressions are not allowed, and yet I assure you they are the only ones I can use!

I love you, I long to embrace you again and again, and kiss you, beloved mother of my joy

Darling, sorely-tried woman, from whose eyes go forth a song of praise, from whose lips words of consolation and help fall so refreshingly! You, aye you, must bow your white head in prayer over our happiness, that it may be blessed! Listen! You must be our teacher that the evil days may not come too soon.

Your son's wife, your own, your faithful
THERESA.

www.ingramcontent.com/pod-product-compliance
Lightning Source LLC
Chambersburg PA
CBHW031747230426
43669CB00007B/516